CRIME
ON THE
CANALS

CRIME
ON THE
CANALS

ANTHONY POULTON-SMITH

PEN & SWORD
HISTORY
AN IMPRINT OF PEN & SWORD BOOKS LTD.
YORKSHIRE - PHILADELPHIA

First published in Great Britain in 2019 by
PEN AND SWORD HISTORY
An imprint of
Pen & Sword Books Ltd
Yorkshire – Philadelphia

ISBN 978 1 52675 478 3

A CIP catalogue record for this book is available from the British Library.

Printed and bound in the UK by TJ International
Typeset in Times New Roman 11.5/14 by
Aura Technology and Software Services, India

Pen & Sword Books Limited incorporates the imprints of Atlas, Archaeology,
Aviation, Discovery, Family History, Fiction, History, Maritime, Military, Military
Classics, Politics, Select, Transport, True Crime, Air World, Frontline Publishing,
Leo Cooper, Remember When, Seaforth Publishing, The Praetorian Press,
Wharncliffe Local History, Wharncliffe Transport, Wharncliffe True Crime and
White Owl.

For a complete list of Pen & Sword titles please contact
PEN & SWORD BOOKS LIMITED
47 Church Street, Barnsley, South Yorkshire, S70 2AS, England
E-mail: enquiries@pen-and-sword.co.uk
Website: www.pen-and-sword.co.uk

Or
PEN AND SWORD BOOKS
1950 Lawrence Rd, Havertown, PA 19083, USA
E-mail: Uspen-and-sword@casematepublishers.com
Website: www.penandswordbooks.com

Contents

Chapter 1   The Canal System 1

Chapter 2   1826 William Hancock 3

Chapter 3   1833 Thomas Bodle 5

Chapter 4   1838 John Thompson 8

Chapter 5   1839 Charles Clark 9

Chapter 6   1839 Christina Collins 10

Chapter 7   1846 William Norman 15

Chapter 8   1847 Ann Bridges 17

Chapter 9   1853 Eliza Lea 20

Chapter 10   1857 John Turner 25

Chapter 11   1864 Thomas Caddick 27

Chapter 12   1865 Matthew Jones 29

Chapter 13   1865 Parkes and Dayus 30

Chapter 14   1867 Henry Thacker 32

Chapter 15   1870 John Goodwin 34

Chapter 16   1870 Timothy Bellingham 37

Chapter 17   1873 Elizabeth Lowke 39

Chapter 18   1874 The Tilbury 42

Chapter 19   1876 Southwick's Iron Foundry 44

Chapter 20   1885 Counterfeit Coin 46

Chapter 21   1888 Charles Snitheringale 48

Chapter 22   1888 Harry Price 49

Chapter 23   1890 Thomas Elliman 50

Chapter 24   1896 Edward Grain 54

Chapter 25   1898 Thacker and Polkey 56

Chapter 26   1899 Percy Horton 59

Chapter 27   1902 Jane Doley 61

Chapter 28   1902 Sarah Foster 64

Chapter 29   1906 Fowl Play 66

Chapter 30   1910 Glynn and Speedwell 67

Chapter 31   1913 Bromwich and Humphries 70

Chapter 32   1913 Catherine Bradfield 74

Chapter 33   1913 Frank Phipps 79

Chapter 34   1913 Williams, Jackson and Collinge 80

Chapter 35   1915 Annie 82

Chapter 36   1915 George Taylor and James Cross 83

Chapter 37   1918 Trippier, Thompson and Downham 85

Chapter 38   1919 Annie Wright 87

Chapter 39   1921 Mary Sutcliffe 94

Chapter 40   1926 William Mulvanny 97

Chapter 41   1927 The Bushells 99

Chapter 42   1927 Olive Turner 100

Chapter 43   1931 The Preston Hundreds 104

Chapter 44   1936 Eliza Worton 107

Chapter 45   1939 Edith Vincent 110

Chapter 46   1949 Pearl Cowman 116

              Conclusion 118

              Bibliography 120

Chapter 1

The Canal System

James Brindley's name is synonymous with canals. Commissioned by the 3rd Duke of Bridgewater, he solved the problem of bringing coal from mines at Worsley to Manchester. Now known as the Bridgewater Canal, it is considered to be the first British canal of the modern era.

Brindley's design made a great difference to canal building in three ways. Firstly, he changed the way canals were built. To him the answer was to reduce the amount of earth being moved and, considering the labour-intensive methods of the time, this made perfect sense. Instead of building embankments he used the natural contours of the land. While this does mean a more circuitous route, it cuts down on the number of locks, thus reducing bottlenecks, and does not result in an increase in travel time. Secondly, he avoided cuttings, preferring to tunnel. This would not have proven popular with boatmen who needed to 'leg' their way through the tunnel as their horse made its way over the top. More importantly, he developed a method of puddling clay, which produced a water-tight clay used for lining canals.

Before long Brindley's improved reputation saw him commissioned to produce other canals. His plan was to link the four largest rivers of England: the Mersey, Severn, Thames and Trent by canals and thus open up the interior to navigation. The coming of the railways put paid to his vision. However one factor, which has largely been overlooked, is his role in aiding the development of the region known as the Potteries. While the ceramics were made prior to the canal, these fragile wares benefitted greatly from the smooth transportation system and continued to do so even after the coming of the railways. Before his death in 1772 Brindley had headed the construction of 365 miles of canal, including the Staffordshire and Worcestershire Canal, the Coventry Canal, the Oxford Canal and many others. He achieved this in just thirteen years.

Trivia and railway buffs across the land will recognize the date of 1 January 1948 as the end of the 'big four' independent railway companies, which were replaced by British Rail. Yet few understand this nationalization of the railways extended to every port on the coast and on the rivers, too. This also meant the nationalization of Britain's canals and shows how these apparently quite unrelated means of transport not only often follow similar routes but also share many aspects of their histories.

Today's airports and ports are highly security conscious. Even standing on railway stations we hear constant reminders to not leave luggage unattended. This is not a modern problem, having been an issue since thirteenth-century custom's officers levied a charge on goods. By the eighteenth century, taxation had risen to a point where smuggling was rife. This era produced the traditional image of the smuggler complete with his ever-present foe of the excise man in tricorn hat and armed with a pistol.

As the canal and river systems were developed, they provided an opportunity for some to make a little extra money. We have all heard how something 'fell off the back of a lorry' and prior to the internal combustion engine, other goods and wares would just as easily have fallen off a narrow boat. Indeed, it was much easier to do so with a boat for the journeys were longer, plenty of quiet spots could be found along the canals and, most importantly, there was a perfect hiding place. A barrel or valuable item dropped overboard en route could be picked up at a later date, providing the place was marked well enough to be found.

Today there are more than 4,000 miles of navigable inland waterways in the United Kingdom. This includes canals, non-tidal rivers, tidal rivers, large lakes, deep lakes, lochs and estuaries. Half of this distance, almost 200 distinct stretches, could be considered to be canals, either purpose-built or canalized rivers. Travelling the canal network in the United Kingdom is tantamount to stepping into a living museum. This museum gives access to 2,700 listed structures, fifty scheduled monuments, and five UNESCO world heritage sites standing alongside the towpath.

Over the last 250 years the canals have seen plenty of crime. Robbery, theft, assault, smuggling, child cruelty, manslaughter and murder have made the headlines over the years. In the following pages, all these and more will be examined. We will look at the stories behind the crime, the locations both then and today, the investigations, the trial and, where applicable, the sentence.

Chapter 2

1826 William Hancock

People of a certain age will recall jocular remarks suggesting any large load was always being moved by Pickfords. This name, synonymous with moving house, is still used for removals and storage around the country. However, few will be aware that the earliest Pickfords' loads were on water, not on wheels.

Zachary Langton, a partner in Pickfords, had employed William Hancock to work as a boatman on one of the company's fly boats. He had been employed for some three or four years when, on 3 August 1826, he was arrested and charged with theft.

Fly boats were forever busy, working both day and night. The following events began to unfold at around 9pm in the evening. Thomas Wise, a porter working for Pickfords, saw a bale of cloth delivered to the warehouse. He noted that it had come from the Castle Inn, Wood Street and was to be shipped to Mr Slater at Knutsford. It contained seventy-six yards of kerseymere, a fine woollen fabric with a close nap, produced in fancy twill weaves and was earmarked for shipping on the Liverpool boat. Wise saw Hancock carrying the bale across the warehouse, something he should not have been doing, and resting it against the door.

Wise then left the scene and went to the clerk, Edward Powner. The two men conferred and, as Wise had suspected, overheard that the package should be heading north for Knutsford, although Hancock's boat was departing in the opposite direction bound for Leicester. Returning to the warehouse he discovered the bale had disappeared. Crossing to the door, Wise saw Hancock carrying the cloth to his boat. In his haste, he dropped the cloth into the water but retrieved it and put it on the boat. Watching him cross back to the warehouse, Wise asked: 'What are you doing? What was that splash?' Hancock said it must have been a block falling into the water, although he had not seen it. Wise and Powner then called the boat back. Not only was the kerseymere discovered there but a second roll was found, this of broadcloth.

Summoning the police, a Constable Moore took statements from all employees working that evening. While nobody had witnessed the second roll of cloth being pilfered, a porter by the name of John Church reported how Hancock had given him a sixpence to 'get a drop of beer'. It was safe to assume it was at this point the broadcloth disappeared. On 14 September, William Hancock was brought before the assizes, charged with stealing nineteen yards of broadcloth worth £15 and seventy-four yards of kerseymere valued at £22. Found guilty, William Hancock was sentenced to be transported for seven years.

Records show he left on 13 June 1827, one of 160 convicts on board the *Layton*. They arrived on 9 October 1827 at Van Diemen's Land, now known as Tasmania. This is the last record ever found of William Hancock. Whether he survived his sentence, returned home or stayed in Australia to begin a new life is unknown.

Chapter 3

1833 Thomas Bodle

Sunday, 1 February 1833 did not turn out to be a good one for boatman Thomas Bodle. As with so many of his profession, he worked hard and drank with equal enthusiasm. After travelling south from Shipley in Yorkshire to London to collect a load of coal for his employer, Mr Munday, he set out that evening to sample the night life, just as businessmen in the capital do to this day.

He started out at the Windsor Castle at around 6:30pm where he drank more than three quarts of porter and a glass of gin. Opposite him a man named Turfrey seemed keen to sell him something. At 11:30pm he moved on to the Macclesfield Arms, where he had another glass of gin and a port wine – once again joined by Turfrey – before being told he had had enough and it was time to sleep it off. After settling his bill, he counted his money and knew he had some eight or nine shillings in silver and one-and-a-half pennies in copper before leaving.

Sleep he did, but in a chair at the City Arms. However, on waking he could neither remember what he had drunk nor whether Turfrey continued to shadow him. Nor could he recall how long he had slept or when he left. Indeed the next thing he remembered was walking over the bridge and feeling rather 'fresh' when approached by Turfrey and a man named Harding. At this point the bemused Bodle seemed to think they were going to escort him to his boat, for even when quite sober in court three weeks later he recalled telling them his boat was at wharf number thirty-three.

Turfrey and Harding each grabbed an arm and marched Bodle off, but only part of the way. Then Harding knocked him down and took all the money from his breeches before throwing him down a hole. Bodle was in too great a stupor to know where he had landed, and indeed, knew no more until he arrived at the station house the next morning.

Luckily for the victim, police officers Epps and Cook could fill in the gaps for Bodle. Seeing him walking between Harding and Turfrey,

PC Epps thought it odd and followed. During this time, the constable heard one of them – he thought it was Turfrey – say how they would 'do him in'. He lost sight of the two men for a while, during which time he sought the assistance of PC Cook, but eventually he stopped Harding and Turfrey and ordered them to help them search for Bodle, although they insisted his whereabouts was a mystery to them.

Despite their denial they soon found him in the cellar of a partially built house and ordered Harding and Turfrey to retrieve him, which they did. With one pocket turned inside out, it was clear he had been robbed and both suspects were immediately arrested. Bodle posed more of a problem and they sent for a cart to carry him as he was making no sense whatsoever, although at that time they could not be sure whether this was due to drink, being dropped down the cellar or both.

Bodle's testimony conflicted on a number of points with those of the witnesses called from the three public houses. Both John Groome, waiter at the Windsor Castle, and Nicholas Lucraft, landlord of the Macclesfield Arms, spoke of Bodle drinking more than the man remembered and, if his singing and conversation were anything to go by, he was much more the worse for drink than Bodle's account would have suggested. Rachel Jones, landlady of the City Arms, even remarked on how it had been Turfrey who had tried to get a room for Bodle as an act of kindness, but she had had to refuse the request.

With Bodle too drunk to remember anything with clarity, PC Epps had quickly seen the danger the man faced and followed as closely as possible without the risk of being seen. This brought the officer within four or five yards of them at one point when he clearly heard the prisoners speak of robbery and murder. Without the constable's testimony it seems 24-year-old John Turfrey and Samuel Harding, 28, would probably have got away with it and Thomas Bodle may well have died that night in the cellar.

The actions of the constable saved one life and arrested two who had stolen the veritable pittance of eight shillings and seven pence halfpenny. Found guilty, both men were sentenced to hang. However, as with more than half of those condemned to be executed, their sentences were commuted. Both men were transported to Australian penal colonies for life. John Turfrey arrived in New South Wales on 3 November 1833 with 299 other convicts aboard the *Aurora* after a journey of four months. Records show Turfrey lived to his sixty-second year, dying a prisoner in New South Wales.

Samuel Harding was one of 280 convicts aboard the *Norfolk,* departing one year and one day later than the *Aurora*, which transferred to the *Lady Kennaway* at Cork on 14 September 1834. It would be another four years before *Lady Kennaway* would travel to Australia, and not with convicts but with those wishing to migrate to this new life. The vessel subsequently left Harding at Haulbowline in County Down, Northern Ireland as he was 'sick'. Whatever ailed Harding would have been regarded as terminal and Harding was left there to die.

Chapter 4

1838 John Thompson

In the latter part of 1838, a vessel belonging to the East India Company arrived in London. On 8 November, a steward from this vessel named John Kennedy delivered two packages and a box to the London offices of Pickfords, which were to be forwarded to Liverpool to be collected by him. Six days later, with John Kennedy now living in Cheshire, he duly collected the goods. That evening he opened them and discovered the box was missing a shawl and several other items.

Next day he reported the goods missing and an investigation was launched. One of Pickfords' clerks had documentation showing the goods moving from London to Wolverton, now part of modern Milton Keynes, where they were collected from their agent Thomas Dakin and brought to Liverpool. He identified the carrier as the boat captained by John Thompson, giving police the address to which an officer went to question the boatman.

Matthew Parker of the Metropolitan Police Force arrived and began to search the home of the accused. However, while doing so his wife rushed upstairs and others in the house blocked his pursuit. Not to be outsmarted, the policeman turned and ran out to the back yard just in time to observe two shawls coming to the ground, having clearly been thrown from an upstairs window. The officer retrieved them and made the arrest.

In court, these were identified as the China crepe shawls belonging to Mr Kennedy. While police had not traced the whereabouts of a number of coins in gold and silver, also missing from the box, they had several witnesses to say Kennedy had been showing similar coins to a number of people in a Cheshire public house. Initially the court adjourned the case, holding the prisoner on remand while awaiting further evidence and despite nothing being found Thompson returned to court to hear a guilty verdict.

In 1840 John Thompson found himself in the penal colony in New South Wales, Australia, transported for seven years. No record can be found of him ever leaving.

Chapter 5

1839 Charles Clark

Law breaking comes in many forms and on 5 January 1839, a rather different canal-based crime was discovered and brought before R. E. E. Mynors Esq at the monthly sessions nine days later.

While we may see the Kings Arms, Alcester Lane End, Kings Norton, Birmingham as a strange venue for a court, inns were not always simply somewhere to quench one's thirst or cut through a juicy steak. Prosecuting was Mr J. Yemen, an officer for the Animals' Friends Society, who had witnessed Charles Clark aboard his boat when it was being pulled by a donkey. Clearly the animal had neither the strength nor the stamina for such an arduous task and he pressed for the maximum permitted penalty in the hope it would act as a warning to others.

Found guilty, a fine of twenty shillings was imposed with Clark ordered to get himself a horse.

Chapter 6

1839 Christina Collins

Monday, 17 June 1839 and at Rugeley in Staffordshire the still-warm corpse of Christina Collins was hauled from the Trent and Mersey Canal about a mile north of Rugeley wharf at a place known officially as Brindley's Bank – named after the famous engineer James Brindley – and at a sharp turn.

Although 180 years have passed since that day, still the climb leading up from the towpath is referred to as the Bloody Steps, stained red by the blood from the poor woman's remains. These steps are cut from local sandstone and erode easily and thus what we see today has been repaired many times. Yet this does not prevent local stories of blood oozing from the rock, believed to be a prelude to the victim's ghost being glimpsed walking that towpath. This constant reference to blood does not fit with the coroner reporting the cause of death as choking and subsequently drowned – no mention of blood being spilled.

But what led up to the fateful day? Why was Mrs Collins travelling alone on the canal? Where was she bound for? In truth Christina's thirty-eight years had been quite eventful since her birth in Nottinghamshire in 1801. Her father Alfred Brown, a spectacularly unsuccessful inventor, still managed to pay for a good education for his daughter.

Reaching adulthood she married one Thomas Ingleby, a Scotsman who earned a living as an illusionist. Aside from his act – which included beheading a chicken and then resuscitating it, smashing a perfectly good pocket watch and then showing it whole and in working order once more, and culminated in him swallowing six (and only six) items of cutlery – he also found time to pen a book on his chosen career entitled *Ingleby's Whole Art of Legerdemain*, published in 1815.

Significantly older than his bride, Ingleby left her a widow on his death in 1832 and she found herself penniless, childless and stranded in Ireland. She managed to work her way back to England and, finally finding true love, married a second time in 1838. As Mrs Ingleby the only excitement she saw was on stage. With Robert Collins she had a passionate and loving marriage but, once again, little money.

As an ostler, Richard struggled to find work in Liverpool and was forced to move to London. He went alone, leaving his wife working for a pittance as a seamstress. During this period, they would have longed for the day they would be reunited. Evidence of the depth of their love was revealed with his cross-examination at the trial. Reports of the time stated he wept openly and loudly from the moment he entered the witness box until he broke down completely by the end.

Eventually he managed to scrape together enough for her to join him in the capital and sent her one guinea (£1.05), the equivalent of two weeks' wages for him. (Note some sources say this was a sovereign or £1.)

So Christina Collins found herself heading south on the Trent and Mersey, leaving Liverpool bound for London. She carried everything she owned with her, two boxes and a bundle all tied with white cord. Boarding a barge at Liverpool on Saturday, she arrived at Preston Brook around midday the following day and there transferred to a second vessel. She travelled with three men on their barge but, as history records, this proved to be a very bad decision. Already men of questionable morals, they freely admitted most of their money came from stealing and, fuelled by an excess of drink, they raped and brutally murdered her before dumping her lifeless body into the canal.

Christina had certainly opted for this craft as it was a fly boat. They answered several problems associated with the standard boats. The fly boat was smaller, with even less room given over to living quarters but the size made it easier to control and thus, with an adequate crew, it could travel both night and day. The boat chosen by Christina was one of a fleet belonging to Matthew Pickford. His company was now a success as the ten initial boats in 1795 had grown to more than 100 by the time Christina Collins chose one as her mode of transport. Not that it was luxury accommodation. Having to keep moving as much as possible meant one man leading the horse and another steering at all times. In the case of this boat, the other two were in the cabin and any passenger, such as Christina, would have had a makeshift cabin in the middle of the boat, most likely only a canvas sheet to keep dry on a bed of straw and known to boatmen as 'the hole'.

Brought to trial were James Owen, George Thomas (also known as Dobbell), and William Ellis. When questioned they spoke openly of theft, taking advantage of any opportunity, chiefly from other boat users. As if this had not influenced the opinions of others sufficiently, they then boasted of never having spent more than an hour in church in all their adult lives.

There were two trials. The first, in 1839, which was unable to reach a guilty verdict on the charge of rape – not surprising as the evidence against them proved circumstantial at best – saw the judge direct the jury to acquit them on that charge and set a retrial for the charge of murder, giving more time for further investigation. At the second trial the following year the prosecution had two other accounts to call upon, that of a fourth individual on the boat and another prisoner who had shared cells with the men on the murder charge at the time of the original trial.

Several witnesses were called, mostly from where the boat stopped to take on refreshment, feed the horse, or waited to negotiate a lock. All those who came forward spoke of the passenger's distress and how she seemed to be anxious, even afraid of what the men on the boat might do. Some said she was weeping, others repeated her pleas to the boatmen to 'Leave me alone, I'll not be tempted to go down with you,' and how she repeatedly called for 'Oh Collins, my Collins!'

The role of the teenager named Musson on board the boat has never been overly understood, neither on the day of the murder nor during the investigation. Remember this was a small craft, a fly boat, where the living quarters would have been cramped for one as the cargo would have taken up most of the room. Assuming Musson played no role in the attack upon Christina Collins, on such a small boat he would surely have heard something. It later transpired he had been leading the horse and was thus some distance ahead of the boat. Yet walk the towpath here today. Even with the noise of traffic in the background and on the busiest of days, there is peace and quiet – exactly what makes travelling the canals the great leisure pursuit it is in the twenty-first century.

Yet the prosecution relied heavily on the other prisoner, found guilty the year before and awaiting sentencing in the cells. This man was Joseph Orgill, a bigamist – during a six-week trip to Ireland he married a local woman despite already having a wife and four children in England. The law did not permit him to give evidence until he had received a pardon for his own crime. Brought into the witness stand he related what he had been told by Owen the previous year. Both had admitted their respective trials were not looking promising for them, Owen had been trembling and said he feared that the hangman awaited him. He went on to reveal how Musson was innocent and how the other two were guilty of the rapes.

Owen also said he had dropped the body in the water, how she had to be killed or she would tell how they had assaulted her. 'She was dead?' asked Orgill. 'Yes,' replied Owen.

On relating this in court, the judge turned to question Samuel Barnet, the surgeon who examined the body at the Talbot in Rugeley. Mr Barnet went to great lengths to explain how the victim's frothing mouth showed the cause of death to be drowning. Marks on her neck also showed that someone had their hands around her throat beforehand. However, this was not the cause of her death and she was most certainly alive when she entered the water. Again the judge asked if he was certain, even questioning his experience, to which the surgeon replied he had more than twenty years of experience and was quite sure such frothing could only be caused by drowning or a lengthy period under the water. Her body was still warm when pulled from the canal so this could be eliminated.

The jury retired to consider their verdict and were gone less than forty-five minutes. Pronounced guilty and sentenced to the gallows, the three men spent the days between their trial and execution at Stafford Gaol. During this period an appeal was made for clemency. Here we should reflect on the circumstances which led to this guilty verdict. In law it is necessary to show beyond reasonable doubt that a person is guilty. Was this really done here? At the first trial the judge had directed the jury to find them not guilty, then held them in custody awaiting a trial on other charges. Note the only real evidence differing from the first trial was that of James Orgill. How reliable a witness was he? This man had been found guilty of bigamy and doubtless would have been transported. Yet inside a matter of days he was looking to receive a pardon and be allowed to continue trading as a butcher. Some have questioned whether Orgill simply did what was asked of him in order to avoid his own sentence.

Early on the morning of the execution the prison chaplain, Rev Edward Rathbone, and the governor visited them and advised that they repent. While Owen and Thomas voiced their refusal, Ellis said nothing. Similarly, while Owen and Thomas read from the Bible, Ellis simply stood to one side and listened, although his illiteracy probably had something to do with this. As their last rites were read by the clergy, it was evident by the occasional tremor in their voices how all three had been affected by this most appalling crime.

Just as they were due to be taken to the scaffold a messenger arrived. Courtesy of Her Majesty Queen Victoria, Ellis had been reprieved, albeit only temporarily. Owen wept openly, while Thomas turned and said to Ellis, 'Bill, if you get off let this be a warning to you as long as you live.' This comment clearly pointed out Ellis as guilty, or so Thomas believed. Ellis later had his sentence reduced to transportation for life.

Having said their goodbyes, the remaining two had their hands bound and a bell heralded their final journey. As the Rev Rathbone continued to read their last rites the small procession walked to the drop. Around Stafford 10,000 pairs of eyes watched from every available spot. Windows, walls, trees, roofs, not a space remained as they climbed the steps without any sign of hesitation.

A noose was placed around each man's neck and as the chaplain spoke the words, 'In the midst of life there is death,' the bolt was drawn back. Gasps from some of the women broke the ensuing silence as the crowd watched two strong men convulse on the end of two ropes. After an hour, two lifeless individuals were cut down, this being the signal for the crowds to disperse, all showing due respect for the departed.

While the executions were carried out outside the gaol, the bodies were buried inside the walls in unmarked graves. The only reminder was two slabs which rested against the wall. These read:

> 'James Owen, aged 39, Executed for Murder, 11th April 1840
> George Thomas, aged 27, Executed for Murder, 11th April 1840'

Christina Collins was buried in the grounds of the parish church in Rugeley. It is marked by a memorial stone, erected some years later and paid for by donations from locals. The inscription reads:

> 'To the memory of Christina Collins, wife of Robert Collins, London, who having been most barbarously treated was found dead in the canal in this parish on June 17th 1839, aged 37 years. (This stone is erected by some individuals of the Parish of Rugeley in commiseration of the end of this unhappy woman.)'

Years later Colin Dexter wrote an episode of *Inspector Morse* for television. He based *The Wench is Dead* on the circumstances surrounding the death of Christina Collins.

Chapter 7

1846 William Norman

Today the fastest permitted speed on the canals is 4mph. Any faster and the wash from the boat will damage the banks. The accepted code of conduct also calls for slowing down when passing moored craft – they could well be cooking, and setting the boat rocking is not good when boiling the vegetables.

Although the pace of life on the canal has always been much slower, the pressure to deliver goods within a decent timeframe nevertheless existed. Just as today, competition meant the most reliable service earned repeat business, thus boatmen were always keen to make good time and conflict was inevitable. While one could never have road rage on the canal, the waterborne version does exist, as in the case of William Norman from 1846.

On the Saturday morning of 26 September, boats were waiting to come through the locks on the Grand Junction Canal at Harefield. As always, the locks were the bottlenecks with just one vessel passing through at a time. It takes a set time to open paddles and allow the lock to fill or empty, thus the fastest and most logical answer, when traffic is passing in both directions, is for boats to use the lock alternately. However, even the most experienced boatman can have the occasional hiccup in the form of misjudging a manoeuvre or taking a little more time opening and closing lock gates, which can lead to frustration for those in the queue.

This would have been even more frustrating when working boats alone and the power source was a single horse. Hence when James Carpenter approached the lock at Harefield to find the cause of the delay, his manner towards William Norman was brusque and hardly tactful. Lock-keeper Sam Jordan witnessed some of the confrontation between the two men who, while working for the same carriers, were still in competition.

When traffic is flowing in both directions, the lock is naturally refilled and emptied by alternating boats. Yet when the boats are all travelling in the same direction, accepted etiquette demands the lock be reset for those following. Hence when the flow is down the slope, after passing through it would be expected to find the boatman had at least closed the paddles and probably the gates too. When ascending, the gates would again be closed at the exit and paddles opened on the gates at the opposite end. In effect, the process would be worked between the boatmen, whether travelling in the same or in opposite directions.

It seems the disagreement between the two men came from Carpenter pointing out the onus on filling the lock had been Norman's. The latter disagreed and before long the two men had squared up and, despite the pleas from George Norman, William's brother, had walked away together to fight in a nearby field. By the time George arrived, testosterone levels had reached a new height, both men had removed their shirts and were already fighting.

George pleaded with his brother to back down, later readily admitting William had been the aggressor and that he had warned him several times as to the dangers of drinking excessively. George received a blow himself while trying to pull the cut and bruised William away. When the fight started up again it had been William who demanded 'another round or two'. In George's opinion Carpenter seemed ready to give up and continue along the canal.

Pausing for breath a couple of times the two fought again and again until William fell backwards and landed on the ground. Propping himself up on one elbow he paused and took a breath before falling backwards. A gurgling sound came from his throat and George thought his brother was fitting. But William Norman never moved nor made another sound for he was dead. James Carpenter did not realize his opponent had breathed his last and so, retrieving his shirt, returned to his boat to continue his journey.

Surgeon Hayes Kidd examined the corpse. In his opinion none of the contusions about his face had been of sufficient force to be the cause of death. An internal examination revealed a massive amount of blood in the brain cavity and the surgeon said this had been the cause of death. He had, in effect, died from his enraged state which had caused the blood vessels to rupture – a condition consistent with those who drank far too much alcohol.

The verdict was returned in minutes: not guilty.

Chapter 8

1847 Ann Bridges

Modern diesel engines give a very different image of early life on the canal when horse power meant literally the horse. These strong beasts toiled long hours but, aside from getting the boat moving initially, the effort required to haul up to 30 tons for a fully-laden boat would not have been overly taxing.

Yet while both the heavy boat and powerful animals posed their own dangers, the greatest menace to those on the boat, and the towpath, came from the long tow ropes. Examine the grooves worn into the brickwork of canal bridges; marks worn smooth by tow ropes pulled taut as the boat was drawn beneath.

When boats pass in opposite directions they pass on the left, which is the opposite side to road traffic in Britain. Hence horses pulling those boats would need to pass on the right to prevent the ropes becoming entangled, with the tension relaxed on the outer ropes to enable the inner boat and horse to walk or drift over the outer rope.

Boats often travelled late into the evening or, more often, made a start before daybreak. Long journeys and tiring hours meant mistakes were made, which resulted in accidents. Such occurred on the Grand Union Canal near Uxbridge on 29 October 1847. Having delivered a load of iron to London, Isaac Bridges and wife Ann were returning north to Tipton Green with a cargo of wheat for the Bissell's company of Tipton. A second boat from the Bissell fleet, the *George*, skippered by Alfred Bridges, Isaac's brother, was following. Travelling in the opposite direction was William Hickman who failed to follow the accepted procedure, with dire consequences.

Hickman's boat, the *Wellington*, followed behind the *Thistle*, which had already passed in the accepted way. Yet Hickman got his line completely wrong and brought his horse on to the wrong side. While Bridges, walking with the horse, managed to bring his rope over the head of Hickman's horse, thus correcting one problem, he could not get Hickman to lower his line despite several warnings. This resulted in the rope dragging across the other boat and, worse still, becoming wrapped around Mrs Bridges' wrist as she steered. Hickman continued on, despite the shouts, as poor Mrs Bridges was ripped from the deck and thrown into the water.

Isaac Bridges jumped into the canal to assist his beloved wife, followed moments later by a rope thrown by his brother Alfred. Isaac shouted out to Hickman to 'Stop the horse! Stop the horse!', which he did but only long enough for the rope to slacken and allow her release and for Alfred to help pull both to the towpath. Ann Bridges was taken to hospital in Uxbridge.

So great was the tension on the rope, it left a deep and wide mark on her wrist. Surgeon William Rayner agreed this had not been enough on its own to cause death, but the shock of being bodily yanked from the boat and the damage done to the whole length of the arm (he used the description 'mortification') had extended to the lungs which, at the subsequent post mortem, were found to be gangrenous.

On 31 October, Police Sergeant Richard Roadknight arrested Hickman. The boatman admitted he was responsible for causing the woman's injury at Uxbridge, that he was also in the wrong for not allowing their boat to pass over his line and for his error in continuing on his way. However, contrary to the statement by Alfred Bridges, Hickman claimed it had been he who had thrown the lifeline to help pull husband and wife from the water adding that, had he not done so, both would have drowned. Thus, he said he should be praised for his actions, not held accountable for her death.

At the subsequent trial for manslaughter on 22 November, Hickman maintained he knew the code of conduct on the canal. As counsel pressured him for a more detailed response he claimed that, while so many knew the unwritten rules, most got away with whatever they could when they could. Predictably this was denied by both brothers but an expert opinion, given by the aptly-named Mr Lock of the Grand Junction Canal Company, made it clear while such may happen on rare occasions this could never be acceptable. Mr Lock brought a copy of the Act of Parliament and accompanying by-laws into court and read of how a fine would be levied against anyone not following these rules.

A second expert, a clerk on the Grand Junction Canal named James Roadknight, brother of the policeman, affirmed the by-laws were rigorously enforced. To his knowledge every station would have a copy of them posted up in the office. Not only would everyone know these regulations but they would follow them to the letter, as failing to do so would incur a fine the boatmen could ill afford to settle.

Hickman had no prior record, was not known to the police, had never been fined for problems on the Grand Junction or any other canal, and a character witness spoke of him being a considerate and conscientious individual. Perhaps most tellingly, neither brother had heard of the man being named as a danger to other traffic. Had this been the case, warnings to be wary of the *Wellington* and its skipper would almost certainly have been heard.

Yet there can be no doubt Hickman ignored the by-laws and as a result, albeit indirectly, a beloved wife and co-worker had died. Hence it comes as something of a surprise to find the accused was not only found not guilty but did not even incur a fine for his ineptitude despite his admission in court. We can only guess at the thoughts of the Black Country man, Isaac Bridges, who returned home to Tipton that winter a widower and also missing a work colleague.

Chapter 9

1853 Eliza Lea

Visitors to Regent's Park, particularly to the area around the zoo, may be surprised to know this seemingly tranquil area was once a murder scene. On Monday, 31 January 1853 the body of 26-year-old Eliza Lea was dragged from the Regent's Canal. She had been drowned.

A lengthy and greatly interrupted inquest, which began on 3 February, pieced together the details of what happened on that night. Coroner Mr Wakley soon requested an adjournment, stating he wanted to bring the case to the attention of the newly appointed Home Secretary, none other than Viscount Palmerston who within two years would be prime minister – albeit the official title did not exist at the time. The minister agreed the accused, Thomas Mackett, could be brought before the coroner's court provided he return the prisoner to Mr Broughton, magistrate at Marylebone Police Court, by noon the same day.

The court viewed the remains of the deceased at the inconsiderately named 'dead house' of St Pancras Workhouse. Meanwhile Mackett, accompanied by two wardens, came from Clerkenwell Prison and was held in a private room and brought into the court only when evidence concerning the prisoner was heard.

First on the witness stand was William Lea, the victim's father resident at number 68 1/2 (yes really!) Augustus Street near Regent's Park. Identifying the body as that of his daughter, he spoke of having seen her on the morning of the 31st at 7am. For the last five weeks she had spent time at their home, arriving on Sunday evening and remaining until Tuesday each week. He next saw her at the Regalia public house in Augustus Street at 11pm, when the police summoned him to identify the woman they had pulled from the canal.

Surgeon Joseph Johnson, of Park Village East, arrived shortly after 11pm. He examined the body of a woman wrapped in blankets on a table at the Regalia and confirmed there was no sign of life. Later examinations confirmed his initial suspicions that death had been through drowning, adding he found no evidence of an attack or of any violence.

Pianoforte-maker Henry Swindon Williams, resident at nearby Henry Street, had been a customer at the Regalia on the night of her death. He had been drinking in the club room and stepped into the rear garden for a breath of air. Within moments he heard the cries and splashing of what he recognized as a woman in the waters of the adjacent canal. At the same time, he heard the footsteps of someone running in his direction along the passage coming up from the towpath of the canal.

He hurried inside to summon the landlord, Mr Rolfe, and together they made for the passage leading down to the canal. Here they met a man and asked, 'What's wrong?' The man replied, 'I think a woman has thrown herself in the water' but, retrospectively, they considered his demeanour was unnaturally calm considering the circumstances. Mr Rolfe shouted at him to 'Come help us get her out!' and together they ran down a passage to the water's edge.

Here they could distinctly hear the sound of splashing ahead of them but the fog was too thick for them to see any further than a few feet from where they stood. The landlord called out, 'Can you float? Can you speak?' but received no response. Rolfe ran for a light and a rope and he was followed by the man they had met at the top of the passage. Whilst they were away Williams heard three splashes but by the time Rolfe returned it was quiet. Then they realized the stranger, having followed Rolfe up the passage, had disappeared and the landlord cried, 'I believe the vagabond has thrown her in the water!'

Williams ran up the passage and along Augustus Street where he met a constable. He asked if he had seen a man dressed in what he identified as the clothes of a bricklayer's labourer but the policeman replied he had not before accompanying Williams back to the towpath. Summoning the assistance of a colleague, one PC Percival, the two constables managed to haul the lifeless body out of the water and took it to the table in the Regalia where the surgeon later pronounced her dead.

A plan of the area was produced for the court, showing the length of the passage as 110 feet. Williams placed himself at least sixty feet from the water's edge when he first heard splashing. After bringing Mackett into the room for Williams to identify, the witness reported it had been very dark and foggy. While he could not say it certainly was not the man he had seen on that evening, he could not positively identify the accused as being present.

When PC Percival took the witness stand he told of how he had answered the summons from his colleague. Unlike his fellow officer, he had seen the prisoner about 11:05pm when he passed by carrying a bag or basket over his shoulder. Within two or three minutes he was at the Regalia helping bring the body of the woman to the bank. This they managed by tying a large stone to the end of the rope then throwing it across the body, thereby drawing it slowly towards them. Together they tried to resuscitate her but it was too late.

Labourer Thomas Mackett, of Ecclestone's Buildings in Marylebone, had cohabited with the deceased for some time. Based on the evidence available, the coroner's court came to the decision that Eliza Lea's death had been the result of wilful murder. Immediately the coroner moved the entire court to Marylebone Police Court in front of Mr Wilding – just as he had agreed with the Home Secretary – where witnesses continued to be called.

Her mother, Mary Ann Lea, had last seen Eliza between 9 and 10am on the 31st as she was leaving their house. Her daughter had lived with the prisoner for almost six years, leaving him five months earlier and supporting herself by taking in ironing. Since she had known the man, Mary said her daughter had been the worse for drink a number of times. Eliza had often said Mackett had mistreated her, claiming he had even threatened to kill her. Despite her mother's pleas, Eliza insisted she speak to Mackett to ascertain whether he intended to do her harm or not. Her mother gave her half a sovereign (ten shillings) to get a parcel of merino wool out of pawn and to buy the trimmings for her that day.

Next, landlady Jane Slater spoke of how both the deceased and accused had lived under her roof as man and wife. She confirmed Mary's testimony and said she had seen the prisoner beat Eliza on a number of occasions. The worst of these was when, having heard the woman scream 'Murder!', she climbed the stairs to find Eliza's nose pouring blood and a very drunk prisoner holding her down on the bed.

Perhaps the one person who knew the situation best was Eliza's friend Sarah Hermitage of Pratt Street, Camden Town, who had known both of them for some time. While never witnessing his mistreatment of her, Sarah said that unquestionably he had beaten her regularly. Sarah last saw her friend on the day of her death at 10:45pm. She had with her a brown paper parcel containing the merino wool, lining, braid, buttons and cotton – a parcel brought into court and identified as that she had carried that night.

Earlier in the day, Sarah and Eliza had searched for Mackett. At Kingston they searched without success but later found him at the chapel in Margaret Street, Cavendish Square. At around 5:30pm they spoke briefly (Sarah could not hear what was said) before all three went to a local public house where Eliza paid for the porter they drank. From there it was on to the Southampton Arms in Camden Town, there they shared a quarter of gin.

From there all three went back to the Hermitage home. Arriving at 7:45pm they ate and drank tea, with Mr Hermitage arriving home at exactly 9:10pm alongside Sarah's brother. Despite her husband's protests, Mackett and Eliza insisted each would sing a song, she opting for the traditional English folk song *I've Wandered by a Brookside*. Sarah declined when Eliza asked her to take care of the parcel and deliver it to her mother next morning, so she took it herself when departing with Mackett at around 10pm.

During the evening Eliza had become agitated when Mackett informed her, 'I was married last Sunday', and she refused to believe it. He insisted he had a new wife and she should leave him alone but she demanded to see the certificate, something he would hardly have on his person. Her disappointment in his marriage seemed in complete contrast to the earlier conversation in the public house where she had purchased porter for them all after he said he had no money. She agreed only on the condition she never had to see him again.

Mr Thompson had a pawnbroker's shop in Manchester Square. On 1 February, the day after Eliza's death, a woman came into his shop at 11am. She pawned a parcel of merino and lining, giving her name as Anne Marshall of 6 East Street. It later transpired she was the new wife of the prisoner but was using her maiden name. She returned to redeem the ticket at 8:30pm that evening, when she seemed extremely anxious and in a great hurry.

Between her two visits to the pawnbroker, PC Bow had visited their home asking for the parcel. She went to retrieve it, returning in no more than fifteen minutes. Earlier, around 1pm, PC Bow had called while wearing plain clothes, telling Mackett his employer had been asking for him. Leaving together the officer then revealed his true identity and questioned him with regard to the evening spent with Eliza Lea. Mackett maintained he had left her at Sarah's home around 10pm the previous evening.

Mackett's statement differed with that offered by Henry Timson, a barman at his father's public house in Mornington Road, the Victoria. He confirmed he had served the couple a quarter of gin. He did not see either leave but, in his opinion, neither could be said to have been drunk. Alerted by the noises coming from the area around the canal and the Regalia, he had recognized her as one of the customers he had served that evening.

Arresting officers reported Mackett had not responded to questioning, and was seemingly in a state of despair. His head fell to his chest until he finally uttered a single sentence: 'I shall be able to clear myself.' After being sent to trial, and bail denied, he again found himself escorted by a policeman. However, this time he would have been quite grateful for his presence for they emerged from the court to find an angry mob of at least 500 surrounding the building.

Friday, 13 May was the unlucky date set for Mackett's trial. He sat quietly and unmoving as the same witnesses and statements were read to the court. Aside from the judge's summing up, the last person to speak was the counsel for the defence. Mr Parry made an impassioned plea on his client's behalf, saying the evidence was at best circumstantial and certainly not enough to convict Thomas Mackett.

The jury retired and returned just thirty minutes later with the verdict – not guilty.

Chapter 10

1857 John Turner

On Monday, 10 October 1857, a boatman by the name of Davis called at the cottage of the lock-keeper at the Old Ford Basin of the Regent's Canal by Victoria Park. Davis walked lock-keeper Robert Russell to a point midway between the lock and the Victoria Bridge, pointing to a mutilated body in the water. Unable to land it where they stood, the two men managed to get a rope around it and towed it along to the basin outside the Horsford Arms public house where they brought it ashore.

For the first time the men were able to get a good look at the appalling injuries. Several gashes around the area of head and neck had almost severed the head from the torso. Clothing had been ripped or cut sufficiently for them to note a serious chest wound. Extending from the chest to the neck, the gash was so deep it had severed the spine and vital organs. None of those present, all of whom were experienced in the operation and ways of the canals, could see how such injuries could ever have been inflicted by a boat.

News of the discovery spread quickly. Before long it reached the ears of mast-maker Mr Bailey. A description of the still unidentified deceased intrigued him, especially when recalling a conversation with his wife Jean. On the previous Wednesday morning at 6am she had answered the door to their brother-in-law, John Turner, who was propped up against the wall rather the worse for drink. She asked him into the kitchen and invited him to sit down.

The Turners were going through troubled times. Jean's sister and John's wife had been diagnosed with a mental illness and he bemoaned that 'my old lady is gone mad' and how he could never go home again. He went out into their yard and sat again where he fell asleep for two hours before Jean invited him in for some breakfast. During the rest of the morning, John spoke quietly of his family's misfortunes and the desperately unhappy home. With his wife insane and an inmate of

St George's Workhouse in Old Gravel Lane, his marriage was effectively over. Their son, an only child, was serving with the British Army in India and could offer no support. While the family were aware that he had spent his every penny on drink in an attempt to erase all memory of his troubles, it later transpired his problems were even worse than he had admitted and he had run up rent arrears of over two pounds. However, after eating a hearty soup for lunch, he appeared to be in better spirits and lay on the sofa sleeping again for a further four hours.

After work, Mr Bailey returned to their home at 10 Tomlins Terrace, Limehouse where he broached the subject of their brother-in-law. He had not been seen by his wife since the previous week; she had tried to find him at home but to no avail. After a brief conversation, both agreed the description of the deceased was reminiscent of John Turner and thus the husband visited the police station. He subsequently identified the corpse of 52-year-old John Turner.

In the twenty-first century, investigative procedures and methods may well have produced very different results than 150 years ago. Yet in the mid-nineteenth century, much of what we take for granted today lay far in the future, hence the initial inquest hearing was adjourned to procure a more detailed report from the doctor. On resumption, the doctor stated that the wounds had been made with a very sharp instrument and a powerful blow. Conversely, these wounds clearly showed they had been caused by a surprisingly small item and one yet to be identified.

This made little sense. The coroner called a second adjournment and ordered a thorough search of the canal to find the mystery implement. By the resumption nothing had been found; indeed nothing ever has. This is hardly surprising considering the distance the body had been dragged after its discovery. That place may not have been where death or the injuries had occurred, and this was a sizeable canal and a very small item.

When asked if he thought it possible the man could have committed suicide by falling on whatever had caused the injuries leading to his death, the doctor agreed it was certainly possible. However, whether such an action could be envisaged was a different question. As a means of suicide, it would have been most uncertain and risked agonizing injuries. Although from the evidence given by the family, he could have been at a low enough ebb to have considered taking his own life.

The coroner recorded an open verdict, effectively stating nobody could be held responsible for the death. John Turner's family remained unconvinced.

Chapter 11

1864 Thomas Caddick

In 1864 the newspapers carried the report of a trial. Whilst we must concede scientific procedures and expertise were rudimentary by today's standards, some of the decisions and evidence from the Christian case seem almost irrational.

For the past eight years Henry Christian, aged 37, and his wife of 35 had lived at the Coppice in Sedgley. Together they were raising their two children, a boy of 7 and a babe in arms. Their courtship had been a brief one, she marrying Christian just weeks after the death of her previous husband, Isaac Jones. This earlier marriage had also produced a child, a daughter now aged 9 or 10.

As Mrs Jones, her life had been hard but blissfully happy. As Mrs Christian, each day had brought little but misery. Henry's brutal treatment of his wife saw her family having to intervene on several occasions until the situation reached a climax on 31 July. He returned home on Saturday night, once again the worse for drink. She reminded him what drink the night before Sunday pigeon racing had done for his brother, as he was found dead in the Tipton Canal not three weeks earlier.

Her warning may have been one of genuine concern for her husband but he did not see it as such. Indeed in his alcohol-fuelled state he lost all sense of rationality and threatened to end the life of both his wife and his stepdaughter and bundled up the bedclothes around the candle promising to 'burn them up'. Fortunately his son managed to wrest the candle from him as his mother and stepsister, both still in their nightclothes, ran from the house into the night. The drunk chased after them, armed with a heavy leather strap, following them to the home of his father-in-law, a 60-year-old shoemaker by the name of Thomas Caddick.

The following night, 1 August, saw no change. Once again he returned home drunk and this time he delivered the warning, quite unreasonably, telling his wife she should change her manner or the marriage would be over. After an exchange of words, he announced he was leaving and attempted to remove the clothes from his own son, presumably to sell and thus buy more drink. Bravely, his wife stepped between them and tried to protect their young son, only to receive a quite brutal kicking.

At this precise moment her sister, Mrs Louisa Millwood, was passing. Hearing the noise from inside she entered the house where she joined in the melee, also incurring injuries courtesy of the now crazed Henry Christian. Close behind followed a third sister, Mrs Ellen Richards, and their father Thomas Caddick.

Immediately Christian focused his attack on the old man, knocking him down and, having trapped his face between his fingers, pressed his thumbs firmly into his throat. The three women succeeded in getting the man off their father, allowing Caddick to stand and stagger outside. Here he met Ellen's husband William Richard and, pointing to his throat, said, 'Will, he tried to throttle me!' at which point he fell to the ground, quite dead.

In December, the case came to court with Christian's defence counsel arguing that his client's actions could never be considered the cause of death as he had walked and spoken afterwards. He continued to argue that it seemed at least as likely death had been the result of a burst blood vessel. The prosecution was unable to counter this argument as the doctor conducting the post mortem, quite astonishingly, had not come to court. Both Christian and Caddick, despite his advancing years, were known to have short tempers. All three sisters conceded their actions had not been ladylike with each of them setting about Caddick united in a single cause.

In his summing up the judge told the jury they had three possible decisions. Had Thomas Caddick died following a fight then the prisoner should be found guilty of manslaughter. Yet had the prisoner been struck first then he had simply been defending himself and should be acquitted. He also offered a third option, albeit a most unlikely one, where his death had been quite unrelated to the fight and a mere coincidence.

The jury returned after a brief deliberation. The prisoner was acquitted but the jury added that they would undoubtedly have been happier with their decision had the doctor's evidence been available to them.

When reviewing the case 150 years on, many of the omissions and the almost flagrant disregard for judicial procedure seem quite shocking. However, on reflection perhaps the omissions are not in the procedure, nor in the reporting but in what was brought to court. Thus, should we be reading between the lines and looking at what had *not* been said to explain that day in court?

Chapter 12

1865 Matthew Jones

On 4 June 1865 at the King's Head public house, Hunton Bridge, Abbots Langley, Richard Bradshaw received a delivery. He knew what the package contained – one shirt and two green plaid handkerchiefs. He left these with Newman Godwin in the tap room of the King's Head. Within an hour Bradshaw learned the items had been stolen. There had been no witnesses but the only person to have left in the interim had been boatman Matthew Jones.

With only one suspect, Bradshaw summoned the police and, accompanied by Police Constable Dunn and a man named William Montague, the latter also having had a shirt stolen, went to Jones' boat on the Grand Junction Canal at Home Park Dock. After asking Bradshaw to wait on the towpath, the officer boarded the vessel and a scuffle ensued. Moments later the constable emerged with Jones under arrest and what were later identified as the stolen items.

PC Dunn later told in court how, having entered the boat, he found Jones lying in the cabin clutching a bundle containing two shirts and two handkerchiefs. Jones resisted arrest, denying theft, while the other man on the boat, James Brough, also claimed to have no knowledge of the items and proved impossible to apprehend until Dunn returned later with assistance. The items were later identified in court by Bradshaw and Montague, with the shirts valued at 2s 6d each and 6d per handkerchief.

In his defence Jones claimed he had no knowledge of his actions prior to his arrest, saying he was 'fresh'. The use of 'fresh', a word having surprisingly numerous uses, is offered as a defence and thus presumably is not used to mean 'vigorous' or 'new'. In Victorian slang the term could be used to describe one's pallor, thus presumably Jones claimed to be feeling faint or light-headed. Charges against Brough were dismissed.

The jury convicted Jones on the charge of theft of the shirt and two handkerchiefs belonging to Richard Bradshaw. The second shirt, belonging to Montague, had yet to be recovered and thus theft by Jones could not be proved. Jones received six weeks with hard labour.

Chapter 13

1865 Parkes and Dayus

Today, cases of driving without care, of driving a non-roadworthy vehicle, or so-called road rage are sadly so commonplace they can hardly be considered news. Yet these are not restricted to the twenty-first century, indeed nor are they only seen on the road, as this court case from 1865 shows.

Saturday, 28 March that year saw Richard Dayus coming through West Bromwich. While negotiating the third in a flight, lock-keeper Richard Parkes approached him. According to Mr W. Carrick, agent for the Birmingham Canal Company, his movement along the canal had been erratic in the extreme. Indeed, lock gates had proven difficult to open in one case and to shut in another. This would have angered Parkes as he was employed to see that canal traffic moved along as quickly as possible.

There was no suggestion of any damage to the lock gates, hence the complaint referred to Dayus' piloting skills, albeit it was not stipulated as such. This would also fit with Mr Carrick's insistence that Dayus had been guilty of having navigated the boat, then in his care, through the canal with neither a rudder nor anyone steering on board. At this point Dayus' counsel suggested removing the helm was commonplace when negotiating locks, but almost all present denied this. It should be noted that the boat would be towed by a horse, not powered by an engine, and the beast would have no control over the direction or orientation of the craft.

With the lock gates effectively jammed, Parkes walked up to Dayus. Witnesses described the confrontation between the two men. For reasons unclear to some Dayus suddenly fell to his knees and, following an unrepeatable oath, was seen to lash out with the windlass he had to hand, striking Parkes. However other witnesses spoke of Dayus having fallen after they observed Parkes landing the first blow, again with a windlass but this to the head thereafter Dayus retaliating in kind.

Having been taken to Queen's Hospital, Dayus was treated by a Mr Thompson, and the surgeon appeared in court confirming the injuries sustained by his patient resulted in him being hospitalized for four days. Dayus was subsequently charged with assaulting Parkes, with Parkes similarly charged against Dayus, with the latter also charged with flouting canal rules and regulations in not being in full control of his boat.

All three cases returned guilty verdicts. Parkes was fined ten shillings plus costs, or twenty-one days in prison. Dayus was fined one shilling for the assault and a further nine shillings for his breach of the Canal Act plus costs, again with the alternative of twenty-one days in prison. Equal fines for these men probably indicated both were held equally to blame.

Chapter 14

1867 Henry Thacker

Possibly not the most famous of vegetables, the mangold wurzel is of the same family as beetroot and sugar beet. It is a modern creation, developed by selective breeding from the sea beet in the eighteenth century. Identified by the large swollen white or yellow roots, its name comes from the German for 'beet' *mangel* and 'root' *wurzel* and it is used as cattle fodder.

Modern mangold-wurzels could also be grown for sport. Mangold-wurzel hurling certainly predates the vegetable's first recorded mention as a crop, hence competitors must have hurled other unnamed roots in the past. By the nineteenth century this sport became popular with farm labourers as it enabled them to stand on an equal footing with their lords and masters – at least for an hour or two. Its popularity reached a high on the Somerset Levels in the early twentieth century, with each village boasting a team.

The rules seem ludicrously complex. After being harvested, a number of mangold-wurzels are piled on a cart in the field where they grew. Here they receive the blessing of the local clergy, before each hurler selects their vegetable. Said competitor then has to stand with both feet in a withy pitching basket and, on the command 'HURL!', launches the innocent root at a target – nothing instantly recognizable as a target, but another mangold-wurzel always known as Norman. Hurling is allowed only with a straight arm; any bending is immediately called 'NO HURL!' by the watcher, an official standing behind the hurler.

The winner is he (for although women did compete, it's unlikely they were ever victorious) who hurls his chosen mangold-wurzel closest to Norman. Any disputed decisions are decided by measuring distances with a willow stick ritually summoned by the umpire's call of 'WILLOW "E"!' With the winner announced and named Mangold King, he has a selection of village beauties called Mangold Maids paraded before him and will select one to be his Mangold Queen.

Boatman Henry Thacker, given as resident in Wolverhampton, found himself in court on 4 October 1867. For three days he had been held on remand, not for the severity of the crime but as boatmen found it all too easy to disappear as indeed he had already managed to do.

Thacker was charged with stealing a quantity of mangold wurzel from a field belonging to James Procter of Pilstone, north of Stafford. This master criminal had managed to avoid capture for a few days, making his getaway aboard the horse-drawn boat after removing the vegetable from the field on 26 September. Thacker had hardly planned this heist in detail for, plying this stretch of canal regularly, he was well known to everyone. Thus, police simply had to await his return and arrest him.

In court Thacker cut a sorry sight indeed. Clearly his three days in a cell had made a big impression and any repetition seemed most unlikely. Even the police stated the Wolverhampton boatman had an excellent record previously and was well-known and well-liked by all on the canal. Rather than sentence the forlorn figure to longer punishment, the bench discharged the prisoner on the promise other boatmen would ensure he made it home safely!

Chapter 15

1870 John Goodwin

Car owners in Britain will tell you that the place comes to a standstill following a snowfall. This is something of an exaggeration, but for the boatmen of yesteryear this could easily be the case when the still waters of the canal iced over and brought the carrier boats very much to a stop. Even a day without work would put a strain on the tight budget of the boatmen. Thus, even in winter months, boatmen would operate seven days a week, including holidays.

On 11 March 1870 a public house in Bath Row, Birmingham was the scene of an inquest. Those present would be asked to decide on the circumstances leading to the death of John Goodwin, a 16-year-old boat boy aboard the vessel worked by William Parker. John, the son of William Goodwin, a farm labourer working near Oldbury, had lodged in Smethwick at the home of Sarah Handley since the end of October the previous year.

On Thursday, 20 January that year John had returned home to his lodgings complaining of feeling unwell. When asked his symptoms, John replied that he feared he was heading for 'an attack of the rheumatism' as indeed he had had two years earlier. He later sent out for two penn'orth of rum, which he drank neat. He complained of feeling unwell on the Friday and on the Sunday, staying at home both days. However, he did work on the Saturday although interestingly not aboard William Parker's boat.

With John's illness showing no improvement, on Monday an assistant of Mr Sutton, a Smethwick surgeon, was brought in to examine the patient. Having complained of an injury to his right thigh, leeches were used to bleed the area. A visit from his father on Wednesday saw John complain of pains in his knee, although William Goodwin took particular interest in the now healing wounds to his lip, which John said were the result of Parker knocking him down and kicking him in his belly, knee, and back while he was down. His concerned father continued to ask about the attack and John told him they had been by the James Iron Foundry. He admitted to making an error when tending to the tow rope, leading to Parker losing his temper and beating the young man.

Later, one Thomas Spinks came forward to speak of what he had witnessed on Thursday, 20 January. He and Samuel Bird, both annealers at the James Iron Foundry, were alerted by a disturbing cry coming from the direction of the canal. On investigation they saw a boy, later identified as John Goodwin, crying as he walked over to the side of the towpath near Bridgeman Street Bridge. Almost immediately a man, one he could not identify later, appeared. The man menacingly said he would 'give him some more', at which the still crying John Goodwin walked over to the boat and boarded her. As the boat pulled away Spinks called out, asking what the man had done, to which John replied he had kicked him.

By the following Thursday, with no signs of improvement, the boy was admitted to Queen's Hospital in Birmingham. On arrival John's symptoms were discussed with him but at no time did he mention a beating while, on the previous day, he had never mentioned anything about rheumatics to his father. The first his father had heard had been from Sarah Handley the day before.

At the hospital Doctor Tolly saw to the patient's treatment. Aside from the swollen thigh he had noticeable fever and, with leeches having no effect, the doctor decided to open up the leg. His fears proved correct for the surgical team found the expected abscess and dealt with it accordingly. For three weeks, the patient remained in hospital, during which time everything possible was done to clear the infection but to no avail, so amputation proved their only option. For a while it seemed as though he was on the long road to recovery but this proved temporary and he died a few days later. The subsequent post mortem revealed the cause of death as blood poisoning.

At the inquest in March, with Parker having been arrested pending an enquiry, the boatman was invited to offer his version of events. Parker spoke of just one event, in December 1869, when he sent the boy ahead to fill the lock and how the deceased had been involved in an accident involving the horse. Whether wrong or right perhaps something of Parker's character was revealed when, by his own evidence, this had been in the gloom and cold at around 4am on Christmas morning.

Parker denied any recollection of the altercation on 20 January and knew nothing of rheumatics.

While the witness Spinks saw the distressed John Goodwin, he had never seen the boy being kicked. Indeed, he could not be sure the man threatening John had been Parker. Without further evidence, nobody could be held responsible for the injury to the boy's leg. There does seem little doubt Parker had not been entirely blameless yet, without proof, the man walked free.

Chapter 16

1870 Timothy Bellingham

On 19 November 1870, a most extraordinary decision was filed by coroner Edwin Hooper in Tipton, Staffordshire. An inquest called to examine the circumstances leading to the death of Timothy Bellingham saw two quite different accounts from the arresting officers and those present.

It never became clear just how or why the confrontation began. All reports begin with two men fighting on the evening of the 16th and two police officers attending. Constable Hunt grabbed one of the men but when PC Crichton reached out for Bellingham he leapt into the canal. Even for experienced swimmers, leaping into water wearing full clothing (including heavy boots or shoes) is most unwise. Thus Bellingham, who it transpired could not swim, found himself fully clothed and struggling in water twelve feet deep at this point.

While his colleague held on to one man, PC Crichton crossed over the canal and waited on the opposite side for Bellingham to emerge. Despite being unable to swim, he managed to stay more or less afloat for five minutes during which time he repeatedly refused to land and eventually sank out of sight. Both policemen insisted they had done everything possible to bring the man to safety but that his actions were 'stupid' and he had refused to help them save his life.

A crowd of witnesses saw and heard everything, among them Mrs Bellingham who witnessed her husband's death. Several gave their version of events, which were quite different from those of the officers. All these witnesses gave more or less the same story of how the police had done nothing to save Bellingham's life. Indeed, not only had they not intervened, they had prevented anyone else from entering the water or throwing a lifeline to assist. It was even said by a man named Hayes they voiced an opinion of how they did not care if he was taken dead or alive.

The jury returned a verdict of 'found drowned'. This meant they were unsure if the pit sinker Bellingham had drowned accidentally or whether, in not coming to the side during his five minutes in the water, he had intended to commit suicide. They acquitted the police of any blame in the matter.

Possibly too much emphasis had been placed by the jury on evidence heard regarding the deceased's background. The inquest heard how Bellingham's father had drowned in the same canal and, just four months prior to this, one of Bellingham's sisters had committed suicide by drowning, again in the same canal at Tipton.

Just how the police officers avoided an inquiry is quite mystifying and would never be allowed today. Furthermore, there is no record of any charge or arrest of the other man involved in the fight. Surely that in itself is significant.

Chapter 17

1873 Elizabeth Lowke

Elizabeth Lowke died in October 1873 at the tender age of 7. She had been aboard a vessel under boatman Frederick Musson, accompanied by Anna Hillman. Brought to Stafford County Assizes in December, the sad story of this young girl's death unfolded.

Aldersley Junction opened in 1772 and allowed movement between the Birmingham Canal Network and the Staffordshire and Worcestershire Canal. Lying at the bottom of a flight known as the Wolverhampton 21 Locks, it had been a vitally important link in the network and once saw very heavy traffic until the Birmingham and Fazeley and Birmingham and Worcester canals eased the pressure considerably. One statistic showing how important Aldersley had been is the count of 20,000 boats which passed through here annually.

On 30 October 1873 one of the many boats arrived and moored up. As it was quite late in the day, Frederick Musson wasted no time in unhitching the horse and walking it round to the stables where he groomed and fed the animal himself. The late arrival was something of an indication of the distance travelled that day and the horse was rewarded for the hard work. Meanwhile dinner was being prepared by Anna Hillman.

Much is said about the overcrowding on these boats. We hear of families numbering double figures living in the confines of a tiny cabin. This is quite untrue although boats may have housed as many as six – two adults and four children assuming they were young enough. Indeed, not only was it impractical but legislation had made any attempt at overcrowding illegal. However, until boatmen were paid a decent wage to enable their families to rent a house, they were forced to live in cramped conditions. When numbers became too great, it was commonplace to ask other boatman to help. These children were expected to pay for their keep themselves by working on the boat. Sadly, many were treated badly.

Several craft were moored up for the night at Aldersley and, after eating, the boatmen and women began to filter away to a nearby public house. This included Musson and Hillman, leaving Elizabeth Lowke alone on the boat. The girl's appearance had been noted by a number of other boaters. Wearing only an ill-fitting skirt, she appeared emaciated and sickly.

When Hillman returned to the boat at around 8pm accompanied by a neighbouring boatman named Tom Mander, they noticed an unpleasant smell coming from the boat which Hillman blamed on the girl. To Mander's distress, Hillman began to beat and whip the poor girl – who was now wearing night attire – as she lay on the floor (her bed) having soiled herself. Next, she dragged Elizabeth from the boat by her hair and, ignoring Mander's pleas for her to stop, yelled how 'the little shit is always doing it.' By the time Mander moved away, Hillman had removed the child's clothing and left her standing naked.

Tom Mander and his family listened to her heart-breaking sobbing until they felt they had to intervene. Mary Mander, Tom's mother, appealed for mercy and Hillman agreed but said she could not speak for Fred who had threatened to kill her and 'toss her in the cut' on several occasions. Mrs Mander helped to clean the soiled child and put her to bed, asking she not tell Musson what had happened. When Musson returned, as ever the worse for drink, he hit Elizabeth hard with the stock of his whip and fell straight into bed and into a deep sleep.

Next morning they found the girl still in her bed and discovered she was cold to the touch. Elizabeth Lowke's miserable existence had ended the previous night. Realizing they should report this, Anna Hillman encouraged Musson to summon assistance. He found an official from the company offices, Charles Millington, and said they had found her dead as they were making ready to leave. Mr Millington enquired as to the bruising around her eye but they told him it had been the result of a fall in the cabin.

Realizing this needed the authorities, both men left to find a doctor and a policeman. When PC Clayton and Sergeant Billet returned with Millington just over an hour later, the clerk noticed the corpse had been washed and evidence of bruising was all over the frail figure. Hillman told the police the bruises were the result of being trodden on by the horse. Officers also discovered an apron covered in blood hidden in the cabin.

Mr John Cook, surgeon, examined the body and his subsequent evidence showed the bruising could never come from the hooves of a horse. However, they were consistent with a beating from the stock of a whip, which had been found aboard the boat. Examinations revealed numerous cuts and bruises, although the internal organs were healthy. Cause of death had been a layer of coagulated blood at the side of her head, which would initially have made the deceased comatose, with death following within a few hours. In his opinion, the fatal blow had been delivered inside the last twenty-four hours.

After the evidence had been produced in court on 8 December, the prosecution spoke of how Elizabeth had been a healthy child when her father had asked the accused to take care of his daughter. He went on to speak of witnesses seeing Musson strike the girl with the stock of his whip on a number of occasions. He conceded the man probably had no intention of killing her but kill her he most certainly did.

The defence counsel argued that there had been no evidence to suggest the accused had done anything more than scold a clearly difficult child – indeed this was undoubtedly the main reason Mr Lowke had rid himself of the burden of raising her. In their defence, he maintained their only crime had been a mistaken idea of what constituted punishment for a child who persisted in repeatedly fouling the cramped living quarters when she was quite capable of using the toilet facilities available.

Following the judge's summing up, paying particular attention to the difference between murder and manslaughter, the jury retired for just thirty minutes before delivering a verdict of guilty on a charge of manslaughter. Jurors were also keen to criticize the father for his awful choice of care, stating he was not entirely blameless in this sad case. Both seemed relieved the verdict had not been murder, which would have carried a death sentence, but their freedom was effectively ended by the sentence of twenty years for each. While Musson had undoubtedly delivered the fatal blow, the judge considered Hillman equally to blame as she had promised Mrs Mander she would cease the beatings.

Chapter 18

1874 The Tilbury

A leisurely trip along the Regent's Canal at Regent's Park ended in tragedy in October 1874. Today's health and safety regulations would never permit cargoes such as those found on the canal that day. The lethal combination involved, then seen simply as 'goods', would be too risky in the twenty-first century.

For years gunpowder had been treated as ordinary merchandise. No special precautions were taken to ensure it was stored or transported safely. Fires were permitted in the cabin – after all the crew needed to keep warm – and they were separated from the potentially explosive goods by nothing more than a wooden bulkhead – even that would not be solid and have at least one ventilation hole. Smoking was discouraged rather than banned, and other inflammable goods such as paraffin and benzoline were carried in the same hold.

Remember this is aboard a powerful vessel, one working hard to convey its load as quickly and efficiently as possible. This is a vessel running under steam power, with a stream of smoke and sparks spewing forth from the funnel as it forges ahead through crowded waters in densely populated districts. This is an accident just waiting to happen.

On the fateful day in question *Tilbury* had been carrying a full load. Among the less volatile goods were a number of casks of benzoline spirit and no less than 5 1/2 tons of gunpowder. A protective tarpaulin covered the hold, tied securely on every side. At the subsequent investigation, both Mr Keates and Professor Taylor pointed to benzoline as a volatile liquid at normal temperatures. It evaporates readily, thus under the tarpaulin a cloud of vapour was readily mixing with oxygen and required little to ignite it.

In the vessel's cabin was a naked flame, be it the fire or a lamp. As the gaseous mixture found its way through the ventilation grille into the cabin it effectively became an invisible fuse between the flame and the gunpowder. Men on other boats reported a bright flash (one description being of 'a blue busticle') and shouted out a warning to slacken off and hold. Nothing ensued and so they waved *Tilbury* on. It was at that point the vessel exploded. Everyone on board died.

In typical Victorian fashion, Government Inspector of Gunpowder Works Major Majendie recreated the explosion for the subsequent investigation. Scaled down to four feet in length, with the taut tarpaulin represented by a tin for the demonstration, it enabled him to show a cork in the benzoline cask did not prevent evaporation. With a candle providing the naked flame it took ten minutes to explode, but explode it did. Benzoline is a fuel, once used in lamps burning a flame. The very properties that made it so useful in a lamp proved so dangerous as part of a cargo.

The Grand Junction Company was severely rebuked for 'gross carelessness'. Parliament was also censured for failing to address the current unsatisfactory and inadequate legislation in the transportation of dangerous materials. Considering how little attention had been paid to ensuring safe transportation, the report did commend the employees and managers for the precautions they took without being required to do so by law.

By the time the report was issued, gunpowder had ceased to be transported by the company, even though a government inspector had pointed to the many times dangerous goods had been transported without incident. Since the accident seventy-five vessels had carried cargoes of naphtha, gunpowder, paraffin, and benzoline. A total 133 tons of gunpowder, including the a single consignment of 9 tons, had been carried over the three months since the destruction of the *Tilbury*, this representing a similar amount to that carried in the preceding three months. Indeed, there was but one difference: the dangerous loads were now charged at twice that paid previously.

Perhaps the worst crime had been ignoring the report a decade earlier when the same suggestions to the government of the day had come following the Erith explosion of 1864 and again in 1865 by Lieutenant Colonel Boxer. The same recommendations of increased safety had been repeated over three years to successive governments. Yet it took the loss of three lives before there had been any reaction.

Chapter 19

1876 Southwick's Iron Foundry

Crime takes many forms. For example, it is often said to be against the law to cycle on the towpath. Yet before you beg mercy from the desk sergeant at the local police station or, heaven forbid, throw yourself on your own sword, this is not necessary.

There is an element of truth in this 'crime', albeit today the worst you can expect is a severely wagged finger for failing to observe good common sense or consideration for other users. In fact, the towpath is not a public right of way and never has been, not even for horses. However, the horse is hardly ever seen on the canal these days, hence there was a period when a permit could be obtained to allow a cyclist to travel along the canal. This was free and it entailed downloading a form from the internet, printing it off, signing it and carrying it with you at all times. It meant nothing and was likely created to prevent arguments as to whether cyclists could or could not take advantage of the largely flat and most interesting routes through the British countryside.

But in January 1876 bicycles were limited to boneshakers and the high-bicycle (the famed penny farthing is an example), neither of which was a problem on the towpath as it would have been quite unwise to have ridden either on such a narrow and uneven surface. Hence it had been something quite different that attracted the attention of a nightwatchman in Birmingham city centre at the Dartmouth Canal Bridge.

Today, alarms and CCTV systems guard properties but once this was the domain of a man who sat all night under an arched tarpaulin in front of a coal-fired brazier and a lamp. In later years these men were employed to watch over roadworks and heard the appalling joke, 'Why's he guarding that hole? Does he think someone will steal it?' countless times.

In 1876 it was Southwick's Iron Foundry which caught his eye. An insignificant door at the rear of the property, which lead to the canal, was ajar, which was unusual. Perhaps today we would see his actions as brave, even foolhardy, but he entered to investigate. Instantly he noticed the strong smell of paraffin and oil, and that long trails of straw, hay and other flammable materials were arranged to enable a fire to spread quickly to reach the upper office area below the rafters. He was carrying a lamp, not an electrical light source but from a flame. If entering a potentially dangerous situation alone was not unwise enough, surely this would be enough to encourage him to make a careful exit? But no, he continued on.

Making his way further in, he saw matches strewn around a large can, evidently the one used to bring in the paraffin. Worse still were the numerous candles, which had clearly been lit with the intention to allow them to burn down and ignite the paraffin-soaked detritus when the arsonist was well away from the scene and with an excellent alibi. Yet the master plan had failed for not a single candle remained alight and none had burned anywhere close to the base. The only explanation was that a chance gust of wind, presumably through the open door, had extinguished every flame.

Had the intended fire been successful, every book, paper and file in the office area would have been reduced to ashes for these, too, had been soaked in oil. Owing to the diligence of a nightwatchman the arsonists failed in their attempt and the perpetrators, always assumed to be the proprietors, were never found nor heard from again.

Chapter 20

1885 Counterfeit Coin

To enable the rebirth of the canals as a leisure industry, armies of volunteers had gathered to clear out the junk of half a century which had accumulated since these arteries ceased to be used to move heavy loads around the country. Some of this had naturally washed and blown into the canal, but not all as the disused canal had also become a dumping ground. It is a far cry from today's modern network, which offers a corridor of the countryside through twenty-first century cities with junctions and basins developed to become desirable living areas. Waterside apartments fetch prices which would astonish those dwelling in the veritable slums of a century ago.

Yet even before Brindley's first canal filled with water, many items had been dropped into the dark waters of rivers and lakes. Some unintentionally fell overboard or were carelessly dropped from a bridge, yet there have always been some which were never intended to be recovered. Just how much evidence lurks beneath the waters across Britain will never be known and, even when recovered, it is highly unlikely a link will be found to a crime.

Canals are dredged regularly, to remove potential obstructions likely to damage the hull or foul a propeller. As any angler can attest, the bottom of a canal may once have been largely flat but over the years the bottom has become littered with rocks and sizeable obstructions where hooks become snagged. The largest of these are as much of a problem for the dredgers as they are for anglers and they're simply too big to remove by normal methods.

Between these rocks must lurk innumerable items dropped by nefarious individuals over the years. Stolen goods impossible to sell on as easily traced thus worthless to the thief and thrown away; perhaps that ring she tossed away after he broke her heart; and the murder weapon long washed clean of blood. Yet sometimes these are found and can be traced to a crime, as was the case with a discovery when cleaning the drained canal near Newhall Street in Birmingham.

It was July 1885 and, between the locks leading out of the city centre, men recovered four bags in the mud at the bottom. They were full of coins and, believing them to have been evidence of a robbery, the men handed them in to the police. However, these were soon identified as counterfeit and recognized as belonging to two fraudsters who were already behind bars.

Two months earlier the men had been brought into Birmingham's courts charged with passing counterfeit coin. Were it not for the evidence found on their persons it seemed likely both would have been acquitted. Clearly, they had attempted to get rid of some of the evidence, possibly intending to reclaim it later, but were now serving lengthy sentences in the harsh conditions of a late nineteenth-century prison with hard labour.

One wonders whether, had the men been set free, the discovery of the bags at the bottom of the canal could have been traced to them and led to a conviction. Is there other evidence at the bottom of the canal ready to prove the guilt of others still walking the streets? Undoubtedly the answer is in the affirmative, although for the vast majority the passage of time will have allowed the culprits to go free.

Chapter 21

1888 Charles Snitheringale

Names are designed to be memorable, to distinguish one animal, plant, place or person from the rest. So, if you are going to have a name, why not make it one people are likely to recognize? As if the unusual name of Charles Snitheringale were not unique enough, to all on the canal network he was simply 'Northamptonshire Charlie'.

On Thursday, 13 December 1888 Charlie was brought before Fenny Stratford Petty Sessions charged with theft. Nine months earlier, on 5 March, evidence suggested it had been he who had stolen one sack of barley, valued at ten shillings, from a boat belonging to Hive and Co of Newport Pagnell. In his defence Charlie maintained his action had been with the knowledge and consent of the boat's captain, William Aldridge, who, although well acquainted with Charlie, denied any complicity in the theft.

It took but moments to come to a decision. Snitheringale was sentenced to three months with hard labour.

Chapter 22

1888 Harry Price

At the coal wharf of Henry Simmonds, in Derby Road, Loughborough, the owner discovered a small amount of money had been stolen. Sending for the police, he and Detective Sergeant Stapleton followed the trail across wet and muddy fields to the canal near Trent Station.

On reaching the towpath the officer saw a boat in the extreme distance and, with Mr Simmonds close behind, set off at his best speed to apprehend the boat and hopefully take the thief or thieves into custody. For two miles the men chased down the boat until it reached Carnforth Lock, the boat having to wait until the lock became available.

Summoning the boat to the side, he boarded and investigated. Boatman Harry Price admitted taking the coal the previous night. 'I'll take the blame,' he said. 'The other two on board knew nothing about it until we got away from Loughborough.' When asked why he had taken it he replied, somewhat predictably: 'I knew there was not a bit of coal left in the cabin.'

Remanded for sentencing, Price reappeared two days later and was given thirty days for the theft of coal valued at 1s 6d.

Chapter 23

1890 Thomas Elliman

Some may consider the inclusion of the Thomas Elliman case to be stretching the boundaries a little. Yet just because the Manchester Ship Canal was still under construction when Frederick Vaughan's body was discovered, it does not make it any less a canal. Not the longest man-made waterway in the country, its thirty-six miles are generally canalized stretches of the rivers Mersey and Irwell. Completed in December 1893, it opened on the first day of 1894.

When planning any canal, the engineers make use of existing topography, limiting the number of locks to reduce bottlenecks and avoid slowing progress greatly. The same is true of roads, albeit to a lesser degree, as slopes are not only difficult to negotiate but are also far more susceptible to erosion. While we see topographical features such as rivers as permanent, if left to their own devices they will change course as levels and currents change, with the river meandering across the lower levels.

Such a change in course had happened a long time ago at Rixton near Warrington. Following a more direct, and consequently shorter, course also meant it could cope with bigger ships and the Manchester Ship Canal can comfortably accommodate vessels up to 600 feet in length. As digging out the route involved many man-hours, water naturally accumulated in the cutting and, somewhat ironically, had to be pumped out. These pumping stations needed to be permanently manned in order to keep them running every hour of every day until completion.

Thomas Elliman lodged at Hollins Green with shoemaker Joseph Arstall. Saturday, 26 April 1890 was not a working day for Elliman and he had taken himself off to Warrington, arriving back on the Saturday evening. Here he showed Arstall a revolver and box of some fifty cartridges purchased that day, saying it would be accompanying him when he journeyed to Australia to join his brother. Next morning Arstall saw Elliman pocket the revolver just before leaving for his latest twenty-four-hour shift at the pumping station.

Arriving at the pumping station Elliman met Charles Bryant, whom he was to relieve, and showed him the weapon. Bryant, concerned that the uncomfortably high temperatures inside the shed could lead to an explosion, advised Elliman that the firearm should be kept outside. Bryant had previously given the same advice to Frederick Vaughan, who also owned a revolver purchased at least twelve months previously and who also had a weapon in his possession that Sunday morning.

Watching the pumping engine for hours on end is unnecessary, Elliman and Bryant passed the time that morning chatting about their respective firearms. It is known Elliman fired off several rounds, even offering one lad a sovereign to stand and let him shoot an object off his head or shoulder. We must take this remark with a pinch of salt as it was undoubtedly never intended to be taken seriously. The only other person to see anyone at the pumping station was a Mr Frank Harris who saw Elliman when passing by at approximately 11:30am but he did not stop to speak.

Shortly before 2pm Joseph Arstall arrived at the shed with Elliman's dinner. He was surprised to find nobody about and very concerned to discover the engine stopped. Arstall soon found his lodger. Lying on his back at the bottom of the cutting, his hat partially covering his eyes and arms raised above his head, Arstall thought he was asleep and called out, 'Hello there! Here's your dinner!' After getting no response, he climbed down and discovered Elliman's pipe a couple of feet away and his friend spread over what must have been a very uncomfortable clod of earth.

Thinking he had fallen he checked for a pulse and found him still warm but with no sign of life. As panic set in he shook the body before looking around for help. At the top of the incline he spotted Vaughan peering out from behind the vegetation and called for help but the man shook his head. Vaughan did not move until Arstall called out for him to fetch the walking ganger (site foreman), a Mr Westhall.

Arriving at the Westhall household he met the son, also employed by the company as clerk of works, and together they went to the police station and accompanied PC Schofield to seek out his colleague. Together the four carried Elliman to Arstall's house. The police officer noted the neck hanging loose and spoke of how he could envisage the accident, Elliman tumbling down the slope after succumbing to heart disease. How he arrived at this conclusion with little evidence and no medical training is quite bewildering.

With Elliman's body back at the house a local woman was sent for – presumably one experienced in such matters – who was charged with removing the clothing and washing the body. Beginning the process of laying out, the unnamed woman suddenly cried out in horror and pointed to a small hole. Together with the police officer, they discovered the hole went through the blue dungaree jacket, waistcoat and shirt, to a tiny circular hole at the right breast where a little blood oozed.

Unable to deal with events of this magnitude alone, the officer sent for his sergeant from Padgate some seven miles away. Sergeant Barnes eventually arrived and announced that the bullet, it being the cause of death, had clearly been fired from a distance – there being little blood, no sign of an exit wound, and no tell-tale powder burn marks on the clothing. Once again this seemed a lot to deduce from very little evidence.

Suspicion immediately fell upon Vaughan and a search ensued. Police investigations led them to the Eagle and Child public house at Hollins Green, where several customers confirmed they witnessed him enjoying a drink around 1:30pm and one said Vaughan questioned him about the distance to Manchester. Later it emerged Vaughan had watched the body of his friend and colleague be carried away as he hid behind a hedge. Witnesses also reported seeing him walking in the direction of Manchester at around this time.

Several details emerged later that day. Most tellingly neither the revolver nor cartridges were on Elliman's person, and a thorough search of the area drew a blank. Surgeon Edwin Jago performed the post mortem and discovered the bullet lodged in the lung. This bullet had not been fired from the revolver of the deceased, but was of a smaller calibre. Contrary to what the police sergeant had said, he thought the gun had been but three or four feet away for the clothing had shown some blackening around the hole in the jacket.

He added there was little evidence to suggest this was suicide. Firstly, the right breast would make a very strange target, it was much easier and more likely to succeed if aimed at the head area. It also seemed odd for the man to have bothered to descend the steep slope, and there was no possibility he could have fallen as fencing and rails along the cutting would have trapped the body. Whilst it could have been an accident this did not explain Vaughan's sudden disappearance. Subsequently his description was circulated to all police stations in the area.

For almost a month Vaughan evaded the police. Indeed, he remained at large until walking into a Manchester police station on 23 May. During the intervening weeks, he stayed at the home of his parents in Ross-on-Wye in Herefordshire. They convinced him to return to the Manchester area and make a statement to the police. On doing so they charged him with manslaughter.

When the case came to court, Vaughan told how Elliman asked him to bring his revolver to work as his colleague intended to buy his own firearm and wished to make a comparison with the model he had in mind. Vaughan admitted it had been his weapon that had shot his friend and colleague but had gone off while Elliman was examining the weapon. Stricken and not thinking clearly, Vaughan disposed of both revolver and ammunition, although he could not recall where.

Supported by the evidence of the coroner, the case against him could never be proven, thus Vaughan was acquitted.

Chapter 24

1896 Edward Grain

On Wednesday, 22 April 1896 shop assistant Edward Grain walked along the canal near Old England House on Radcliffe Road, West Bridgford. It was 8am and, nearing his place of work, he recognized a tiny body in the canal. Clearly far too late to save the life of the child, he sent for the police who removed the small bundle from the water and took it to the Trent Bridge Inn where the coroner held an inquiry that afternoon.

An examination resulted in the report being read to the court. The deceased was a baby girl, thought to be just four or five days old at most. Fully developed and showing clear signs of having lived an independent existence outside of the womb, the only external marks were a pressure mark on the lower right side of the jaw and another to the forehead, both occurring prior to death. Internally the organs were perfectly healthy, there was no damage to the brain, and while the skin on the forehead was filled with blood and thickened, the cause of death had been suffocation. However, it had been impossible to determine how this had occurred.

Turning to the jury, the coroner commented on the increasing number of children's bodies in the canal in the Nottingham area and how this increasingly common problem should be of great concern to all. If the jury agreed, they should instruct the court to pass the case to the police and endeavour to trace those responsible, bringing them to court to account for their actions. Yet the jury returned an open verdict and considered there to be no hope of finding the mother or any others responsible.

To be fair Edward Grain had little to do with this case. However, his name has been used simply because no other was cited. This is perhaps the most poignant factor in this sad case for while we have no idea of the name of the individual, it seems likely the mother never gave her daughter a name either.

Interestingly, eighteen years later an almost identical report recorded finding another child in the canal at Stretford. The age was estimated at about three weeks and this time the verdict was recorded as manslaughter. Death was said to be due to neglect, and not drowning, as the baby could be shown to have died before entering the water.

While the latter verdict may be different, manslaughter by persons unknown still meant the culprits were never sought and not apprehended. We should be thankful in the twenty-first century for medical records, science and DNA.

Chapter 25

1898 Thacker and Polkey

On 30 July 1898 Inspector Agar stood on a bridge crossing the Grand Union Canal at Loughborough. Beneath him passed a boat marked as one of the fleet belonging to the Nottingham Canal carriers Fellows, Morton & Clayton Ltd. Almost immediately the boat pulled to the side, where boatman John Thacker hopped off and made his way up to the bridge and headed south along Meadow Lane. What caught Inspector Agar's eye was the package carried by Thacker, which was quite clearly a weighty one. He decided to follow.

Thacker turned left along Clarence Street, eventually entering the shop of Charles Polkey. Despite the glass in both door and windows, the policeman could see nothing until a woman exited and left the door open behind her. Now he saw two men in a room at the rear of the shop. A man he recognized as the proprietor held a bag into which boatman Thacker tipped something.

When Thacker emerged moments later he still carried the bag brought from the boat, although it was now clearly empty. He was also seen pushing something into his waistcoat pocket. The inspector allowed the man to continue east along Clarence Street while he took himself into the shop and through to the back room where he asked, 'Hello Charlie, what's the boatman brought you?' In reply Polkey pointed to a sofa, and said, 'That bit of sugar and he's coming back for it in a few minutes.' When asked what he paid for it, Polkey denied having handed over anything, neither money nor goods.

Certain Thacker had returned to the canal by way of the next bridge, the inspector set off in pursuit, taking the evidence with him. His suspicions proved correct and he caught up with Thacker at Kendrick's Lock. As he was weighed down with sugar this was no mean feat, although it transpired that both men had well outpaced the boat. He told him what he had observed and at first Thacker denied it, saying he had delivered a bag of clean washing from Leicester. He quickly changed his tune when he saw the game was up, begging him not to lock him up and even suggesting a bribe should he turn a blind eye.

Ignoring his pleas, the two men went inside the cottage of the lock-keeper, a Mr Kendrick. Here Thacker again suggested he could get the inspector 'anything he liked' if he would only 'make it up'. However, he soon admitted he had been taking a boatload of sugar from London to Derby, stopping off to give Polkey fifty pounds of sugar for which he received four shillings. Thacker spoke of how he would take up to twenty boxes marked with the word 'Tate', a name still synonymous with sugar in the twenty-first century. When the two men emerged from the house, the boatman called out to his wife aboard the boat (as she had caught up) to steer the boat to the side. However, it seemed the stress proved too great for her as she was said to have 'swooned' and proved herself incapable of directing the boat to the side.

Thacker was locked up that day, with Polkey arrested the next despite insisting upon his innocence and how the bag would be collected that day. This, of course, would now be impossible with his accomplice in a holding cell. At the hearing two other witnesses came forward. The first, Harry Whitehouse, had also been on the boat.

Whitehouse officially resided at the North Lock in Leicester, although spent most of his time employed as a boy on the barges. He had helped with the loading of the sugar, aboard the boat known as *Nelson* and captained by Thacker, at the canal basin in London. On the return journey he was told to get a loaf of bread from a shop near the Duke of York in Loughborough. Furthermore, he was to ask the owner if he was straight and whether he required any sugar. This he had done and returned with a reply in the affirmative.

In an attempt to discredit the witness, the defence counsel pointed out that young Master Whitehouse had no knowledge of wrong and right. He also addressed the boy's education saying he had only attended school 'for a bit. About three weeks in all'.

Frederick William Fellows, a manager of Fellows, Morton & Clayton Ltd, was also called to give evidence. He reported how he sent the *Nelson* to London where, after delivering its load, it collected 200 cases of Tate's No 1 sugar and 100 cases of No 2, along with two barrels of resin on 24 July. He saw the sugar unloaded on reaching Nottingham. Each barrel should contain one hundredweight of sugar and yet twenty-eight cases were light, missing between two and six pounds each. He could see each had been opened for, even though they had been closed expertly, the packing paper inside was crumpled, something impossible with a full load.

In total, they were missing a little over 100 pounds of sugar and the fifty pounds sold to Polkey was valued at seven or eight shillings. He had no idea where the other fifty pounds had disappeared to, although it seems safe to assume this had been sold off in a similar manner earlier along the route. It should be noted that Mr Fellows also spoke of Thacker's previously clean record, having been employed by his company for more than ten years. It had been down to thirty years of service on the canal prior to this – always with his wife on board – that he had been considered for the position.

Both men were given bail at £30 and, when the case came to court in October, Thacker pleaded guilty but Polkey not guilty. The judge sentenced both men to four months' hard labour, taking trouble to point out that while Thacker's theft was the more serious crime, his sentence took into account his previously good record and his age of 68 years.

Harefield Lock today, where testosterone flowed freely in 1846.

Above left: It still takes a little patience to get boats through Harefield Lock.

Above right: Darley Deep at Uxbridge.

Imagine finding a rope wrapped tightly around your wrist yanking you from the boat and into the waters of the Grand Union Canal.

Above left: The Regent's Canal alongside Prince Albert Road, London NW1.

Above right: Regent's Canal near Old Ford Basin.

Old Ford Road crossing the Regent's Canal.

Grand Junction Canal at Abbots Langley.

Above left: Newhall Street flight in Birmingham, now much redeveloped.

Above right: Lock at Fenny Stratford.

Northamptonshire Charlie would not have been a stranger to the locals at the Red Lion on the lock side at Fenny Stratford.

Above: Canal near the former Trent Station in Loughborough.

Right: Canal at West Bridgford, the modern low water level showing how easily a small body could be hidden in the depths.

Fellows, Morton & Clayton is still a name seen on the canal today.

The bridge on the Nottingham Road crossing the canal where Thacker's boat would have paused long enough for Thacker to hop on to the tow path.

Polkey's shop would not have been dissimilar to this building in Nottingham on the same road today and very near to his establishment.

Above left: Royal Military Canal opposite Mount Street in Hythe, perhaps the metal parts of the purse still lie on the bottom.

Above right: Mount Street, Hythe.

There is plenty of room at the Sharpness Docks in Gloucestershire today.

Some sizeable vessels dock still at Sharpness, and in 1910 these were very busy waters indeed.

Above left: 16 Stratford Street, Coventry would probably still be recognized by its earlier occupant, Enoch Athersuch.

Above right: 67 Eden Street, Coventry where Frank Phipps lodged in 1913. Number 67 is the nearest building of this row of tenement houses.

Rochdale Canal at Todmorden and the lock.

Irlam Street, Manchester is unrecognizable today.

Old Hall Street, Liverpool, where regeneration means little would be recognized today.

Left: Great Howard Street, Liverpool where regeneration has eradicated all but this short stretch of the original street.

Below: John Gulson School, George Street, Coventry – where boatman, Charles Bromwich, was encouraged to send his children to be educated in 1913.

Hoghton Arms, Withnell, Lancashire, where little has changed.

Above: Hoghton Arms, Withnell.

Right: The former Orton Brothers cycle shop in Friar Gate, Derby, where Ronald Light purchased his infamous bicycle.

Above left: Amazing to find the Orton Brothers cycle shop, which now sells second hand goods, has a green bicycle for sale in 2016.

Above right: St Peter's Church at Gaulby.

The fence adjoining the neighbouring field were Light claimed to have repaired a puncture and spoke to a stranger.

Ronald Light would undoubtedly have passed along this road on that fateful day a century ago.

Right: Spinkwell Close is a reminder of Spink Well Lock on the Leeds and Liverpool Canal at Bradford.

Below: A view down Prospect Street, Bradford where the difference in canal level is evident.

One of the stones which lined the Leeds and Liverpool Canal is more or less in situ nearly a century after the canal closed.

Mountford Street, Sparkhill, Birmingham where most of the houses are as they were when the attacker, Charles Grimshaw, set off for Bradford.

The bridge on Lodge Road no longer crosses the canal, which today ends almost seventy-five yards away.

Right: Minworth, Birmingham, where the original houses are long gone.

Below: The front in Teignmouth where Witherington was arrested in 1939. It will have changed in eighty years but not unrecognizably so.

The houses on the right were where the Witherington family lived.

Left: A modern road sign but a long-standing street name, which was home to the Witherington family.

Below: New St George Church at Stalybridge and its graveyard with Pearl Cowman's unmarked grave.

Chapter 26

1899 Percy Horton

At twenty-eight miles in length the Royal Military Canal is unusual because, as the name suggests, its main purpose has always been a military one. Completed in April 1809, this brainchild of Lieutenant Colonel John Brown was built as a defence against Napoleonic forces and designed to prevent any advantage gained from a bridgehead at Romney Marsh.

The defence never saw military action but did prove useful as a control against smuggling. Today the path alongside it forms part of the Saxon Shore Way, a long-distance footpath passing many pillboxes from the Second World War and the ingenious acoustic mirrors used to focus sound from across the English Channel – an early warning system against enemy aircraft. Flying low may have brought them under the radar, but it could not prevent them from being heard by this most simple of systems.

It was a warm 17 July in 1899 at the grocery shop of Mr John Snoad as the owner put together the deliveries for that day. Percy Horton, his 16-year-old delivery boy, set out to bring these to the customers. Working through the list that morning eventually brought him to Twiss Villas at Hythe in Kent.

Just before his arrival at number sixteen, the lady of the house, Mrs Ellen Gravener, emerged to go shopping. As soon as she came out of the door clutching her purse, she realized she had forgotten something. Turning, she placed the purse on the outside window sill and re-entered the building. Young Percy followed behind and left her order in the kitchen before departing. When Mrs Gravener came back outside she discovered both the purse and its contents were gone.

Rather than going straight to the police, Mrs Gravener, who knew the boy's mother, headed straight for his house in Mount Street. Mrs Horton had seen her son a short while earlier and, after listening to details of the suspected theft, went straight to his room where a short search discovered £3 8s hidden, exactly the amount missing from the purse. Now the police were summoned and Percy Horton arrested.

When questioned by Detective Drury, Percy admitted stealing the purse. It had been an impulsive act, one he regretted moments later and he had felt nothing but shame since. In his panic he had removed the money from the purse and thrown the latter into the nearby Royal Military Canal. An appearance before the magistrates next day saw him remanded awaiting trial.

When the case came to court in early August, the bench heard his guilty plea and also a letter from his employer, John Snoad. Whilst he could never condone theft, he could vouch for his otherwise unblemished character during the eighteen months in his employ and said he would be happy to continue to employ him. In court a neighbour also spoke up. Mr Hislopp also pointed to a previously excellent record and said he saw him as an honest individual.

The court dealt with the case under the First Offender's Act, issued a caution and bound him, his mother and Mr Hislopp over in the sum of £10 each.

Chapter 27

1902 Jane Doley

Murdered on Monday, 22 December 1902, 40-something Mrs Jane Doley had lived apart from her family for over a year. Her husband still lived at their home in Wood Street, Wolverhampton together with the youngest son, who had recently left school, while his elder brother was abroad serving with the British Army. Since December 1901 Jane had lodged in a Stafford Street house, paying her way from her meagre earnings as a prostitute.

Labourer Edgar Jenkins found the body. Walking along Southampton Street, near the premises of the Great Western Railway Company, he noticed a pile of untidy sacks in the gloom of the morning but, on lighting a match to examine them more closely, saw that it was the body of a woman. Edgar had no doubt she was dead; her hair was matted with blood and cuts and bruising could be seen to her face. She was still wearing a frozen expression of sheer terror.

He ran for the police, returning with Captain Burnett, Inspector Purchase, and PC Morgan. However they were not alone as the news had spread around the local community. From the canal, the lodging houses, the back-to-back houses, the ale houses, and the women working alongside Jane, there gathered a sizeable crowd who were all clearly in a state of shock. Even the most hardened of policemen were sickened by the sight of the battered and dishevelled body found alongside a corrugated outbuilding splattered with her blood. Nearby lay a black straw hat, later identified as the victim's, and a silk handkerchief of the kind associated with boatmen.

It took three hours before the body could be moved onto the mortuary cart, and another twenty-four hours before Mr R. A. Wilcock opened the inquest, only for it to be adjourned pending further evidence. Jane Doley, her identity confirmed by her husband, had been well known in the area as was her widowed sister with whom she would often be seen sitting outside the church wearing her only possessions. Fellow lodgers told how often she would go hungry and almost never had any money on her person.

While poor Jane received a pauper's funeral, police continued their investigation and, with interest heightened by her burial, there came news of a major breakthrough. An indication of this close-knit community's reaction to this atrocity can be gauged by its willingness to accept a normally distrusted police force into its closed world. It was this door-to-door investigation which resulted in shoemaker Thomas Nash telling of overhearing another lodger, Martin Brown, speak of having killed a woman and was at a loss to know what action to take.

Promptly arrested and subsequently brought before the coroner's court, Brown denied having seen Jane on the day in question, although he had kept company with her, especially at times when he had received his wages from his job as a labourer unloading coal from the boats. Normally he and Jane drank together at the Four Ashes Inn but that day he had visited the Barley Mow and had not seen the victim. He had no recollection of speaking of killing her, nor did he know why Nash would accuse him of doing so. Nobody could make any sense of the accusation and, with no evidence available to help prove anything, an open verdict was reached.

Two years later, with still no conclusion to the investigation, one Thomas Green came forward to provide some interesting evidence. This former soldier had been home on leave at the time of the murder. Thomas and Jane had known one another for about five years, even when she was still living with her husband. After leaving the Army, Thomas Green had been working the boats and had only recently returned to his home in the Wolverhampton area.

On the evening before the discovery of her body, they had been together in the Little Swan public house drinking until 10pm before retiring to his home in Old Mill Street. At around 1:45am he had escorted Jane back towards her lodgings where, standing beneath a lamp, he saw a man he recognized. This was Peter Kelly, who whistled to Jane and they went off together. He never saw Jane Doley again.

After telling this story to several boatmen word reached the ears of the police, who invited him to the police station to make a statement. In February 1905, Kelly was arrested and two days later, on Thursday 16 February, he appeared in court charged with the murder. However, once again British justice could not be satisfied that there was any real connection and a second suspect had to be released.

To make matters worse, Thomas Green had now been arrested on assaulting another woman named Edith Holloway. It later transpired this assault had no direct connection with the Jane Doley case, except that Holloway had accused Green of Jane's murder and repeated this to anyone who would listen. Eventually Green snapped and struck her in a street full of witnesses because of the provocation and the long-time bad blood between them (Holloway accusing him of being the main reason for the breakdown of her marriage and subsequent poverty). He received only a fine but as he was unable to pay, he was locked up.

Over a century later Jane Doley's killer has never been identified. Only two people knew for certain – the victim and the murderer.

Chapter 28

1902 Sarah Foster

Several crimes in this book remain unsolved due to lack of evidence. It seems implausible that, thanks to the advantage of modern technologies, the guilty could have walked free in the twenty-first century.

While DNA identification is now a relatively simple process, it wasn't until the late 1980s that it was used as a tool in fighting crime, and not until comparatively recently did the length of time it took to yield results come down to close to twenty-four hours. Fingerprint evidence, seemingly used in every crime story ever told, was not used at all in this country until July 1901 and then only by the Metropolitan Police Force. It took several years for the rest of the country to catch up. Thus, when a body was discovered in the canal at Ancoates in Manchester on Sunday, 23 February 1902, fingerprinting did not figure as part of the police investigation. The victim was aged about 35, about 5 feet 2 inches in height, was described as fresh of complexion and had brown hair and blue eyes. She was found in the water still wearing a black straw hat (described as trimmed with ribbons in black and heliotrope) a short brown jacket, a black skirt and black knitted stockings. Among her possessions was a purse containing 10.1/2d, a brooch, a pawn ticket, and half an ounce of twist tobacco. Doctors found bruising to her left eye, although this did not appear recent, and an old scar to the left side of her forehead which they hoped may lead to her identification.

Police took the pawn ticket, which was dated 27 January 1902, to Porter & Sons of Corporation Street. Here a woman named Ethel Davies had pawned a shawl and she was immediately traced to her home by Detective Sergeant Jakeman. Miss Davies accompanied them to Fairfield Police Station where she made a statement. It seems she had pawned the shawl on behalf of a married woman named Sarah. She did not know her surname but she lived in Knowsley Court off Charter Street, with her husband Fred. Both Sarah and Fred, a scaffolder, were well known in the Angel Meadow area.

Interestingly, other individuals came forward in response to the description and gave her surname as both Manion and Sweeney. However, the information gleaned from Miss Davies and other witnesses showed her true identity to be Mrs Sarah Foster.

Near where the body had been recovered, a dark well-worn woollen overcoat lay at the foot of a telephone pole. All police found in the pockets were two pipes, one of clay and another of wood with the bowl carved into a head, and two leather patches of the kind worn across the palms of the hands of bricklayers when handling bricks.

Lock-keeper Edward Smith gave a detailed account of events that night. A little after 10:30pm, while standing at his front door in Leech Street talking to the lock tender, his youngest daughter came to the door and told him of a man 'killing a woman' on the canal bank. Their house was built on the bridge straddling the canal and the window in the living room gave a clear view along the towpath as far as Ancoates Bridge 200 to 300 yards away.

Initially Mr Smith took little notice of his daughter as boatmen arguing with their wives on the towpath was a common occurrence. He remained inside to finish the conversation with the lock tender. Meanwhile, his wife had accompanied their daughter onto the bridge to witness the quarrel, with Edward joining them a short while later. They told him of how they had heard a female voice cry 'Murder!' and 'Oh, you brute!' but peace soon returned and all returned indoors.

Moments later the lock tender returned quite agitated. He spoke of seeing a man climbing the telephone pole fixed on the canal path to the side of Leech Street Bridge. Other witnesses later spoke of a man fleeing the scene, although none managed to prevent his escape. Albert Plant, night inspector for the Rochdale Canal Company, had also seen a man scaling the telephone pole around 11:30pm. A woman gave a statement to a PC Bentley of having heard a scream and the shout of 'Murder!' twice. This appeared to be coming from the area between Union Street and Leech Street bridges. Furthermore, as she was standing on the bridge to the rear of the lock house, the man saw her watching him and he disappeared beneath the Leech Street Bridge.

The following day an unnamed man was arrested but released within twenty-four hours. To this day no one has ever been charged for a crime, which may never have been committed. With no forensic evidence to show otherwise it could well have been an accident.

Chapter 29

1906 Fowl Play

Occasionally crime can bring a smile to those reading the account in the morning newspapers. This undoubtedly would have been the case for the people of the Black Country when perusing the columns on Tuesday, 10 July 1906.

Reports of the theft of a number of fowl from Bilston came to the attention of Wolverhampton Police. They also learned the culprits were residing in the Monmore Green area of Wolverhampton and thus, having contacted a local officer, discovered the wanted men were to be found on the canal. Having reached the towpath they spoke to a group of people and one gentleman pointed to a canal boat moored a short distance away and said the men they sought had hidden themselves away after being tipped off as to their likely arrest.

Followed by an interested crowd, two policemen made their way along the towpath and leapt aboard to apprehend the thieves. Unfortunately, the men had outsmarted them and were among the group following them (and included the kind gentleman who had supposedly revealed the men's hiding place). Very quickly the two police officers found themselves locked in the cabin of the boat and a good couple of buckets of water were poured down the chimney, thus preventing them from starting the engine. The boat was then untied and pushed away from the side to strand the now angry, and not a little embarrassed, police officers.

Delighted with their efforts, the crowd dispersed amid great guffaws of laughter. So amusing was the tale, it was told again and again and eventually found the ears of the police, whereupon the long arm of the law reached out and made the arrest of one man, albeit rather later than originally intended.

Chapter 30

1910 Glynn and Speedwell

Not all canal crimes end in the spilling of blood or siphoning off of goods for personal profit. When it comes to *Glynn* versus *Speedwell*, the story is a far more familiar one. Indeed, had the two vessels in 1910 been two road vehicles in 2010, there would be little chance of the case making the newspapers.

In Gloucester County Court on Wednesday, 9 February 1910, in front of Judge Ellicott, James Ffrench of Castlebridge County Wexford, owner of the schooner *Glynn,* sued the owners of a tug owned by the Sharpness New Docks and Gloucester and Birmingham Navigation Company in Gloucester named *Speedwell*. Damages sustained through a breach of the agreement made in relation to the hire of said tug resulted in repairs totalling £300.

On 8 October the previous year *Speedwell* had been towing *Glynn* from Sharpness but it was not alone. *Speedwell's* load also included two lighters ahead of *Glynn* and a longboat and an empty lighter astern – a 'lighter' is a flat-bottomed boat used for carrying heavy loads on canals. Experience was required to pilot such a long load, albeit five craft in tow was by no means unusual.

Having arrived at Price Walker's wharf, the *Speedwell* untied the *Glynn* and the rear vessels to bring the two lighters at the front, which were both heavily laden with timber, to the wharf. After turning back, the tug picked up the *Glynn* and the lighters and the journey continued as instructed by the pilot on board. However, one of the timber-laden lighters had swung across the canal at an angle. While *Speedwell* found the gap, *Glynn* was badly damaged. Accusations were levelled at the *Speedwell* of going too fast on the crowded canal, with the collision blamed entirely on a lack of due care.

The schooner, *Speedwell,* had had a pilot on board since Sharpness – even today a pilot is an expert on local waters and is responsible for bringing in the largest ocean-going vessels to the docks and harbours. Witnesses said the vessel had been steering at 4mph when the mate alerted them to the possible danger of the lighter swinging out across the canal. Several called out to the *Speedwell* to stop but to no avail and, despite the skills and knowledge of the pilot, a collision had been almost unavoidable.

However, less understandably, the *Speedwell* continued on at a steady speed, making no attempt to slow or stop. James Crosby, the mate on the *Glynn*, spoke of how the speed had been the main factor in causing the damage. A slower speed meant the fenders could absorb the impact but, at a breakneck 4mph, the fenders were as effective as if he had 'thrown his hat in to absorb the impact.' However another experienced boatman aboard the *Glynn* shifted all the blame on the pilot, Albert John Davis. In his opinion the accident could have been averted had he heeded the warning shouts and he had ample time to slow and even stop.

Albert Davis maintained that there had been plenty of room in his opinion. He said the problem had been the result of the *Speedwell* canting out (moving sideways) forcing him to steer hard a-starboard and at such time she may have 'smelt' the ground (grazed the bottom of the canal) making the vessel more difficult to control. With the lighter still swinging out and *Speedwell's* steering unreliable, in the pilot's opinion nothing he may have done could have helped avoid the collision.

Clement Lucas, master of the *Speedwell*, agreed. He thought there was sufficient room for both vessels and had followed the pilot's orders to the letter. Lucas added that he thought whoever had been steering *Glynn* had not followed his tug's course but had allowed it to swing across and thus had been the cause of the collision. While the lighter had swung across the canal, he did not apportion any blame to those responsible for both the craft and its load of timber.

Charles Cornock had been in charge of the lighter. He assured the court that no blame could be apportioned to himself or anyone connected with the lighter. While he admitted his craft had swung out, he insisted it had been nowhere near enough to cause the collision as evidenced by one man leaping from the wharf to the vessel. In his opinion, the entire blame lay with the pilot whose local knowledge had apparently failed him leading to *Speedwell* 'smelling' the bottom and canting out.

Leaving the courtroom, the judge consulted with the assessor. On their return, Justice Ellicott ruled in favour of *Glynn* for, in his opinion, had the pilot steered properly there would have been more than enough room. He had learned that the fixing of the ropes was the responsibility of the pilot, not the tug master, and thus the port bow lacked both check rope and bridle and had been unsafe. Therefore the pilot, and only the pilot, could be held responsible with both the damage repair bill and loss of earnings awarded to the tug.

Interestingly no further record of Albert Davis working as a pilot is found. As this is an expert role only for a specific area and based on local knowledge, it is virtually impossible to move elsewhere and thus it appears Albert's career on the canals came to an end after his day in court.

Chapter 31

1913 Bromwich and Humphries

Think of crime and our thoughts turn to the taking of possessions or perhaps of a life. Yet not every crime committed is so blatantly obvious. What about trespassing, a driving offence, noise problems and, in the modern era, those associated with computers and the internet? The same is true of historical crimes. Graffiti on the pyramids would surely have been a problem for the Egyptians and, in the Edwardian era, a major problem for canal families came in the form of legislation insisting their children must attend school.

On Friday, 30 May 1913, Alderman Maycock, Mr T. B. Bethell, Mr S. Gorton and Mr J. M. Scott listened as several individual cases were brought into court. The defendants, all boatmen, were summoned to answer the charge of not providing a reasonable education for their children. Mr A. E. Robinson, the superintendent attendance officer, had rightly brought these cases to court and yet as the facts were revealed, it transpired that not everything was quite as clear-cut as it originally seemed.

First Mr Robinson spoke generally of how the children were not only stopped from attending school but were also made to work on the boats. On the bench Mr Gorton remarked on how appalled he was to see the law so deliberately flouted after long and lengthy debate had resulted in legislation clearly designed for the benefit of the children to provide them with an education.

First brought to the stand was Charles Bromwich. Mr Robinson pointed out he had visited the boat of Mr Bromwich on two occasions, on 22 November 1911 and again on 28 August 1912. Having consulted the attendance book, he discovered none of the Bromwich's three children had a single attendance mark between those two dates. Here it should be noted that the attendance book would be kept by the boat, not the schools. Boats were constantly on the move and never at the same school for long. Thus, with any number of schools near the canal network being funded to take the extra pupils, the onus had been on the canal boat families to bring their children to these schools.

Marking the attendance book not only showed the boatmen had fulfilled their obligation but that the schools would receive a sum to cover their costs. Schools kept their own records and occasional cross-checks were made to reduce the chance for either party to cheat the system. This basic auditing was cited by Mr Robinson, when challenged by the clerk of the court, as to how he could prove the children had not attended school.

The clerk, however, was not satisfied that this would constitute actual proof, especially when Mr Robinson admitted the last time he had seen the attendance book had been August 1912 and this had been brought to court in May 1913, some nine months later. Mr Robinson pointed out that he had visited the boat just four weeks prior to coming to court, when he had been unable to examine the attendance book as Mr Bromwich had maintained it had been left on another boat.

Still the clerk refused to accept this as proof. Surely the defendant simply had to deny the allegations in order to avoid being found guilty. Here Mr Robinson reported how Mr Bromwich freely admitted the children had never been to school. Thus, the clerk turned to Mr Bromwich and asked why his three children had never had a day's education in their lives. Somewhat predictably the response came that the boat never remained anywhere long enough, a few hours moored up at most.

Mr Robinson pointed out they must attend school and, around that part of Coventry, they could walk in to John Gulson School, Red Lane School, or Wheatley Street School – the latter offering special facilities for canal boat children. He also spoke passionately of how the committee had gone to great lengths to ensure these children had the option of an education and continued to provide this opportunity for every child both in and passing through their area.

Offered the chance to explain why he had failed to ensure his children had attended school and how he would make sure they did so in the future, Mr Bromwich stated that he was 60 years old and no scholar, although he could see how no one was of any use on this earth unless they were a scholar. He also repeated how his boat would only be stationary for a few hours at a time and during the school hours this was a maximum of three hours when loading and unloading. To wait while the children were in school was not an option. On a good week he only earned £5 – sixteen shillings of which went to the hire of his two boats – on top of which he had to pay for stabling, the keep of two horses, and toll fees, this leaving barely enough to feed them.

The bench called Inspector of Canal Boats, Mr W. H. Clarke, to offer some satisfactory answer to the problem. Surprisingly he blamed the canal boat operators for the problem, stating that the only sensible answer was to employ men only on the boats, paying them a decent enough wage to enable the rest of the family to rent a home where the children could go to school regularly. The family income could then be supplemented by the wife working, normally in a cottage industry.

Turning to the defendant, Alderman Maycock explained that while he understood the problems faced, the law stated his children must attend school. In reply Mr Bromwich promised he would send them to school but expected the children to come back to the boat as soon as he was ready to continue along the canal. Mr Bromwich was fined 2s 6d plus costs.

Next the court heard the case against Thomas Humphries. This was an identical situation where three children were on board the boat and none of them had ever attended school. Again, the logistics of their attendance was offered as a defence but, despite being sympathetic to the problems, the fine was the same at 2s 6d plus costs.

There were only three children on board the two boats in each case. Often, we hear how these boats had families numbering in double figures and this is simply untrue. While there are many images showing more than five people on a boat, these are posed for the camera. Inside the cabin a board opened out to create a double bed for the parents (if you can call a bed three-feet wide a 'double'), two small children shared an even smaller 'bed' with the eldest having the luxury of a 'single' on the floor of the cabin. Larger numbers were not only impossible to house but also illegal and this is highlighted by a case from 1884. Here the living conditions of those on board were typical of the very worst kind, and one of the main reasons legislation had attempted to address and remedy the problems.

In June of 1884 George Smith wrote of how, in the last fortnight alone, he had seen four distinct examples of why the Canal Boat Act Amendment Bill should be rushed through to enable the authorities to take action against the awful squalor and allow the women and children to free themselves from the situation, which had resulted from a century of inaction.

First, he cited a nearby boat where a man, woman, five children, and a 'chap' were living together and how smallpox could be seen to be 'raging'. Since he'd first noted the situation the 'chap' had vanished and other boaters, seeing him making notes, had voiced their opinions on how awful it was that the filth of the cabin and its dreadful disease had been allowed to float upon the surface of the water used by others for washing, cooking and drinking. They believed this was how the disease had spread, although there were fresh water stations on the canal at the time.

Next Mr Smith referred to a boat belonging to a south Staffordshire firm plying between Wolverhampton and London. Here a man, his wife, their two children, another woman and her three children, another 'chap' and a dog – he counted this as ten, thus including the dog – were confined to a cabin not ten feet square. The third boat he spoke of saw a boatman of 57 years of age, his daughter in her 30s, who had three children by her long-gone husband and two others born after he had left, all in occupation. Finally, in the last forty-eight hours, he had witnessed a string of five boats, where fifteen men and women lived together with seventeen children of both sexes, none of whom had ever attended school in their lives.

George Smith simply highlighted a problem which, almost thirty years later, had yet to be solved. Eventually the families did manage to move away from the crowded cabin to a home on the land. Their children did receive an education and first the railways and latterly the roads saw an end to this lifestyle which had endured since the latter half of the eighteenth century.

For 150 years the canal boatmen hauled large loads around the country. There followed almost fifty years of neglect, before canals saw a new lease of life as the growth leisure industry. We can only guess at what role they will play in the future.

Chapter 32

1913 Catherine Bradfield

Christmas 1913 was just two weeks away. While talk of Yuletide celebrations could be heard on everyone's lips, it will never be known if Catherine Christine Bradfield had been looking forward to spending the season with her family, for they dragged her mutilated body from the Leeds and Liverpool Canal and a murder investigation ensued.

In the twenty-first century we perhaps see the career woman as a modern figure. Yet the 40-year-old Catherine certainly fitted this profile a century ago. She lived in lodgings at 82 Old Chester Road, Birkenhead with Miss Mary Holden. Her landlady later spoke in glowing terms of her paying guest, saying she was an efficient, kind and conscientious woman who had not entertained a gentleman friend since staying with her. She would travel to her place of work at 86 Old Hall Street in Liverpool. This was one of two premises owned by her brother John and had been her place of employment for eight years, initially as a typist and at the time of her death holding the reins as manageress. Catherine had another woman working alongside her in the office and two men were in the stores also producing twine. This proved an excellent second string and complemented the tarpaulin manufactory run by her elder sibling at 68 Great Howard Street.

When, that December, Francis Robinson attempted to open the lock gates, he noted an obstruction and, using a boathook, retrieved it from a depth of around five feet. As soon as the sack came into view he knew exactly what it was and sent for the police. When PC Christian arrived, they could both see the sack contained a body, so tightly had it been tied. They knew it was a woman from the foot and ankle protruding wearing black stockings.

A post-mortem report found no water in her lungs, thus she had not drowned and was already dead when she entered the water. It took no medical knowledge to see she had died a violent death. She had two black eyes, a star-shaped inch-wide hole above her left eye which exposed bone, a second less severe injury just above it and a nearby glancing blow, all undoubtedly caused by the same blunt instrument. The defensive wounds to her hands proved she had resisted and done so for some time as her scalp had so many lacerations they could not be counted.

The motive was assumed to be robbery, as she carried around £4 on her person at the time – an amount described as 'paltry' by the press despite this being more than three times the average weekly wage in the United Kingdom at the time.

The post mortem also revealed that her outer garments were torn and her undergarments were described as 'disarranged'. Newspapers carried reports of the continuing investigation and, in the language of the time, said: 'Suggestions of other more degraded motives were noted but on these points police naturally keep secret.' How times change.

Following the formality of an inquest, the police investigation, led by Detective Inspector Leach, began interviewing co-workers and witnesses. Dockyard labourer George Black and foreman Thomas Crossland both told of how, the previous evening, they had met a youth with a brown moustache pulling a handcart with an obviously weighty load. He had said he wished to drop the rubbish on Lock Fields. Officers also scrutinized the mile between the factory and the canal lock and discovered marks to corroborate their story. Furthermore, the route took a track alongside the railway where it crossed the canal and several large stones had clearly been removed. There had been no need to search as these were already in the police's possession, having been found in the sack used to weigh down the corpse.

A similar handcart, found at the victim's place of employment, showed some staining which may have been blood. Half a dozen mats had been scattered on the floor covering similar staining while lying nearby were two pieces of metal, one part of a shutter, the second unidentified. The policemen spoke to the secretary, Miss Venables, who informed them that all four had been working late the previous evening – she and the deceased at their desks and both men in the stores stamping coal bags. Owner John Bradfield arrived at around 6pm and, stayed for some thirty minutes. He went after ordering they could not leave until the job was done.

By the time the owner returned around 10:45 next morning, Miss Venables had not seen Catherine Bradfield and had already received two telephone calls from Miss Holden, her landlady, worried as she had not returned home the previous evening. When asked how they had gained entry, the two male employees stated that the keys had been entrusted to them by Miss Bradfield the previous evening as she had told them she would be late the next day.

The only other place John thought his sister could have been was with their married sister, Mrs Jacques. He gave the younger employee, 18-year-old Samuel Eltoft, sixpence to cover the train fare to see if Catherine had spent the previous night there. While Eltoft returned with no news of Catherine, Miss Venables pointed out two very evident scratches on the man's face which had certainly not been present the previous evening.

John Bradfield checked the drawer for money. It was empty and yet he knew his sister had collected almost £10 over the previous couple of days. It was common knowledge that when such an amount had been amassed she would bring it to him in her satchel. Mr Okill, who managed the tarpaulin factory, would accompany her when bringing the money to her brother but only when between £10 and £20 had been collected. The aforementioned bag and her watch from the drawer were also missing. By the time the police were called the body had been found. John identified the badly mutilated body as that of his sister, still wearing the brown coat and green skirt she had sported the previous day.

Statements were taken from all those present. In the storeroom Eltoft answered every question put to him but, tellingly, his colleague had disappeared. Images of 23-year-old George Sumner were circulated. Employed here since 1909, Bradfield took him on after he'd worked at a boy's home. He was always a reliable employee, used at both premises as required and his diligence and hard work had been rewarded with an increase in salary to £1 per week earlier in the year. However, money had recently gone missing and Sumner was being watched.

With his image in the newspapers and the case making headline news, a number of lookalikes found themselves being asked to help police with their enquiries. A tramp from Bradford probably enjoyed spending a night in a warm cell, a London man was no doubt less appreciative, while the rumour of Sumner found stowed away on a transatlantic liner was probably started deliberately.

In fact, Sumner had never left Liverpool. Heavily disguised, wearing spectacles and quite different clothes, he had taken lodgings in St James

Street. Here he befriended an Australian sailor named Ronald Bethune and the two spent most of the next week going to picture houses and pubs, all paid for by Sumner. At one point the murder had been discussed by the two men and the landlord of the pub, which had a copy of the newspaper showing the wanted man's picture. Sumner expressed his disgust at the crime but he was so well disguised neither man saw the likeness. Indeed, Bethune failed to recognize him later but did concede he found it unusual that a man he hardly knew could be so generous to a stranger.

It took ten days for the police to find Sumner. When arrested by Police Sergeant Morgan he said he worked at the docks and gave his name as Albert King, but he was unable to prove it saying his insurance card had recently been stolen. Soon after he changed his mind but maintained his innocence. Evidence against him began to mount when Catherine's silver watch was found on his person, while blood stains were present on his grey suit.

When asked for his version of events on the night of the murder he said she had given him the keys and asked if he would open up next day as she would not be there before 9am. He had accompanied her as far as Cotton Hall where she handed him some letters to post, keeping one to a Mr Griffiths which she intended to deliver by hand. He also claimed there had been a mystery third man in the shop that evening, yet nobody else mentioned him and in the close confines of the small space there was nowhere for anyone to hide.

With mounting evidence the police charged both Sumner and Eltoft. Magistrates refused bail and after four weeks on remand the two men came to trial at Liverpool Police Court in January 1914. Another witness had since come forward, one the prosecution was keen to hear from for he had been standing in Old Hall Street on that fateful evening.

Employed as a steward on board the *Empress of Britain*, Walter Musker Eaves had arranged to meet his young lady at 7:30 that evening when she finished work at the tobacconist's on the corner of Old Hall Street. As usual she had been late leaving work and, as young men are wont to do, he ambled up and down the street nearby. As he passed the Bradfield shop, a shutter fell from the window damaging his hat and resulting in a glancing blow to his head. A man emerged and he spoke sharply to him, pointing out that shutters should be firmly closed on such a windy night. While he admitted he would find it difficult to recognize this individual, he certainly recalled the thin-faced Sumner in a grey suit, dark green cap, and dark overcoat who followed behind the first man. The second man had been shown the damaged cap and offered two shillings as compensation, despite Mr Eaves pointing out it had cost more than twice that amount. The man apologized and gave him the money from a white cash bag before both went back inside.

Standing to one side under a street lamp to inspect his damaged hat, a bump interrupted his thoughts. Turning he saw a lad with a handcart emerging, although did not notice if there was anything on it. Almost immediately he saw the man identified as Sumner emerge and, once again, showed him the damage to his hat and received a second apology before heading off in the same direction as the handcart.

When it came to the defence counsel, the lawyers took pains to point out the rope used to tie the body in the sack was of jute, while inside the shop only Italian cord and hemp had been available. Sumner refused to give evidence but Eltoft happily took to the stand, although the latter's answers were quite ludicrous and contradicted virtually all his earlier statements.

The jury retired but were back within fifteen minutes. Both men were found guilty of wilful manslaughter. George Sumner was executed at Liverpool Gaol on 26 February 1914, with Eltoft sentenced to four years. Many thought Eltoft's role had been a minor one and he had been treated badly by both Sumner and the justice system. He appealed but this was dismissed in July 1914 and he served his sentence.

However, this was not the end of Eltoft's tale. In August 1914 the police let it be known that they had overheard a conversation between the two prisoners while Sumner awaited execution. As the police went to great lengths to insist the men could not see one another and were overheard, this suggests the 'meeting' had been organized in order to listen in. Neither man admitted their part in the crime. Indeed the general theme saw Sumner accusing Eltoft of being a traitor and his cross-examination had certainly done nothing to even hint at his colleague's innocence.

However, one interesting thing emerged, which dispels any idea the conversation had been falsified. During the conversation Eltoft revealed where he had hidden his share. Police went to his room and, after unscrewing the top of one bedpost, found money wrapped in a ball of paper. His share amounted to two crowns – a crown being five shillings.

Chapter 33

1913 Frank Phipps

Life on the canal was not easy but, despite what other stories in this book may have you believe, not everyone was a scoundrel – or worse. A report in the *Coventry Herald* on Friday, 30 May 1913 shows how, sometimes, desperation can get the better of anyone.

An allotment at Stoke alongside the Coventry Canal had suffered raid after raid on its produce. One particular allotment holder, 67-year-old Enoch Athersuch, had suffered more than most. Hence when he was on his canal boat moored near the allotment and he witnessed the theft of rhubarb to the value of sixpence, he summoned the police. The officer had no problem finding the thief for Frank Phipps was known to, and had indeed helped work the allotment with, Mr Athersuch who gave his address as 16 Stratford Street.

In the courtroom Phipps pleaded guilty but, after a change of heart, Mr Athersuch said he longer wished to press the case, adding how it was due to the many incidents in the past and on other plots as well as his, that he had reacted the way he had. The magistrate's clerk, seeing the plaintive seemed rather unwell, asked what he did for a living. Mr Athersuch responded: 'Nothing now. I am worn out.'

Phipps, another man who was suffering hard times, was bound over to keep the peace for six months.

Chapter 34

1913 Williams, Jackson and Collinge

March 1913 and three men were brought into court to answer charges of theft from a canal boat. The boat was the *Pansy*, captained by Harry Williams of Irlam Street, Newton Heath and he and his mate, Thomas Jackson of Elizabeth Street, Hyde were charged with the theft of grain. Marshall Collinge, a butcher of Lower Callis, Eastwood near Todmorden, was charged with receiving goods known to be stolen.

For the prosecution Mr Hosegood, who was representing the Rochdale Canal Company, explained that the company had suffered a great deal from theft in recent times and was determined to do something to stem the losses incurred. Over a number of years, the grain loaded in Liverpool arrived light when delivered around Yorkshire. Although suspecting a little had been taken from every sack and despite intense scrutiny, discovering the truth came about by accident.

Purely by coincidence the manager of the Todmorden depot had been at Lower Callis on the Monday evening when he spotted the *Pansy* tied up at the side. As he watched, two men emerged – later identified as Williams and Jackson – carrying between them a sack of oats taken from the boat's hold. Within a few yards they were joined by a third man – Collinge – and together they carried the sack into a field adjoining the canal. By the time the manager arrived and challenged them, they were caught emptying the contents into a fresh sack.

They attempted to take it back to the boat and insisted this had been an extra sack inadvertently collected at Liverpool. However it was later shown that the 'extra' sack had been created by taking a little from the other fifty in the hold. The verbose Mr Hosegood pressed for the severest of penalties for the men. Collinge was particularly in his sights for, as he rightly pointed out, without the market thieves would find it most difficult to make the risk worthwhile.

Williams and Jackson received thirty days each, with hard labour. Collinge, coincidentally the only one of the three to be represented by counsel, could not be conclusively proven to be aware the goods were stolen and thus was only fined £5.

Chapter 35

1915 Annie

Annie does not have a surname because *Annie* is the vessel central to this story. In a Glasgow court on Tuesday, 19 January 1915 all the details of the events of 19 December the previous year came to light.

On that day, *Annie* struck something beneath the waterline while travelling the Forth and Clyde Canal near Lambhill and in order to minimize resulting problems her skipper ran her aground. Doing so prevented her from sinking and becoming a nuisance to other vessels, while also making the retrieval of her cargo an easier task. What he also should have done was place a guard on her as during the night many men (and it later transpired many women, too) arrived to help themselves from the boat in what the prosecution described as 'an act of piracy'.

Although the charge suggests 'a great many', there were just nine individuals in the dock on that day in court. The accused were outnumbered and even outweighed by the evidence retrieved and displayed in the court. This included provisions, clothing, general merchandise and a barrel of whisky littering the court and valued at £43. However, this was a small fraction of what had been stolen and, presumably, just a handful of those responsible.

Four people pleaded guilty: Thomas Ferns was given three months with hard labour; Neil McBride was given sixty days and Alice Kelly and Agnes O'Brien received twenty-one days each. Perhaps they would have been better pleading not guilty as the other five were acquitted.

Chapter 36

1915 George Taylor and James Cross

A battle line had been drawn across Europe. Trench warfare at its most horrific was only twelve months old and, despite the optimistic noises, the Great War would continue for another three years. Back in Blighty, life went on and not always for good, as evidenced by two unscrupulous characters working on the Manchester Ship Canal in Salford in 1915.

Employed by the Manchester Ship Canal at Salford Docks as an assistant delivery clerk, 39-year-old James Roskell Cross earned the princely sum of thirty shillings per week. In 1915 a craftsman commanded a daily wage of five shillings and thus Cross could hardly be considered a pauper. On 11 May, a motor lorry arrived at Salford Docks from a business in Eccles New Road, Weaste owned by George Edward Taylor aged 47. Produce merchant Taylor had been behind the wheel on this day and had collected and loaded thirty bales of cotton.

However, although seemingly an ordinary business transaction, one of many seen at the docks every day, this had been anything but. Unfortunately for Cross and Taylor, the cotton's disappearance had already come to light and the dock police arrested Taylor. With the alarm raised, Cross slipped away but was soon apprehended. Just a few days later both men appeared in court, where each made some quite astonishing statements.

The facts seemed straightforward enough. Cross had produced false documentation to cover the stolen cotton, said to be valued at £260, and had received a cash payment of £183 from Taylor in return. Inspector Clarke of the Dock Police gave evidence saying how, when arrested, Taylor had stated he thought the trade was a legitimate one just like all his other dealings with Cross. Previously all their transactions dealt with oil. Taylor also maintained the price paid equalled the full market price, having told Cross he could never be involved in anything 'shady'.

When the defence counsel questioned Taylor, it seemed the two had already decided the verdict would be guilty. Thus, began an extraordinarily choreographed question and answer session, where Taylor began by claiming he thought it quite proper for men in such positions as Cross to sell goods for their personal benefit. He went on to explain how every ship at the docks had 'always accumulated that for which there was no owner.' Additionally, he understood it customary at both Manchester and Liverpool ports to hand over what he described as 'accounts and overplus cargoes' to share between the men unloading the vessels.

A representative of Parr's Bank, who was called as a character witness, said Taylor had a substantial balance in his account and was regarded as an upstanding and straightforward businessman. Other clients of the bank, with whom Taylor had had regular dealings, spoke of his honesty and integrity. This conflicted with a witness called by the prosecution who, currently negotiating a deal valued at some £480, described Taylor as 'too credulous'.

In closing the defence, counsel pointed to Taylor's previously unblemished record. The jury was told it should also consider that the goods were found on a lorry quite plainly marked with his client's name and taken to a warehouse also showing ownership by Taylor. Surely any fraudulent transaction would never be committed so openly? As an astute businessman, if Taylor was intending to defraud, surely he would do so away from the area of the docks? Thus, rather than finding George Taylor guilty of theft, he should be viewed as naïve and 'a credulous fool'.

In delivering such a defence, he and Taylor had condemned Cross who had already declined to give evidence. Both men were sentenced to nine months in prison with no possibility of appealing.

Chapter 37

1918 Trippier, Thompson and Downham

In May 1918, with the end of the Great War in sight, Appleby's Transit Company Ltd continued shipping goods along the canal network. For decades Appleby's, millers in Liverpool, distributed to sub-depots along the Leeds and Liverpool Canal, with less frequent bulk deliveries heading further afield.

At the beginning of May, a bulk load of Indian corn was heading for Enfield in Middlesex aboard a vessel 'captained' by 30-year-old Robert Thompson, although he was the only member of the crew. Hours later he moored the boat up near Pinnington Hospital in Hoghton. Here he met Joseph Trippier aged 39, a licensed victualler and farmer, who was accompanied by 58-year-old farm labourer Albert Downham, employed by Trippier.

Unknown to the three men, they were being watched. A police sergeant and his constable observed them unloading sacks of corn from the cabin of the boat and stacking them on the towpath. As it was poorly lit at this early hour, it was difficult for the officers to count the number of sacks. Hence when the men left, carrying one sack with them, the police went to investigate and found another sack in the cabin and five more on the side of the canal. A short distance away they discovered a truck containing a single sack of corn, its markings matching those on the towpath.

Later that morning they arrested Thompson and Downham, and Trippier was taken into custody before the day was over. On 25 May, they came to court. Trippier, who owned the Hoghton Arms in Withnell, Lancashaire, a farm and associated outbuildings, denied any involvement after the police officers present admitted they did not see his face but recognized the man through his considerable bulk and his gait. Officers also spoke of his response during interview when he said, 'Alf [Downham] was there but you have no proof I was there.'

Unfortunately, when making this statement Trippier did not know both Thompson and Downham had admitted to their part in the theft. Thus, even though he claimed he had been bedridden with an illness all day, in saying Downham (whom he referred to as 'Alf') had been present he, too, must be implicated.

Downham admitted to aiding and abetting his employer in the theft of seven sacks of corn valued at £15 and received a custodial sentence of two months. Thompson pleaded guilty to theft and the court sentenced him to three months. Trippier received a sentence of six months with hard labour, not only because he was the organizer but also because he pleaded innocent.

Hard labour was certainly well named. Day after day the men would be used to work quarries, build roads, even labour on docks – anywhere where back-breaking toil could be found for them. Trippier should have considered himself lucky for until 1898 hard labour also involved toil within the prison. One punishment being the treadmill or treadwheel, where the prisoner initially provided the power to turn the wheel and grind flour, which provided the prison with an income. Later this involved simply turning the wheel with no end product. Others were given the crank, a handle to be turned several thousand times a day that could be tightened to make it harder to turn.

Such seemingly pointless exercises are long gone but have left their marks on the language. We still speak about returning to work, particularly after a lunch break or holiday, as returning to 'the treadmill', while in the vernacular of the prisoners, guards are known as 'screws'.

Chapter 38

1919 Annie Wright

Along with the Christina Collins case this is perhaps the best known of all canal crimes, albeit it is usually referred to as the Green Bicycle Mystery. Initially the death of Annie Bella Wright (who was known as Bella) had been considered a cycling accident. Yet when a most attentive police officer made a thorough search of the area, he found a bullet partially buried in the dust. Miss Wright had been shot. What followed proved a long and most frustrating investigation.

Annie Wright, aged 21, lived with her parents at Stoughton in Leicestershire. Described as an attractive, well-built girl, she always cycled to and from work and was 'keeping company' with one Archie Ward, a stoker in the Royal Navy, who was expecting to be demobilized in August 1919. However, it was common knowledge that she had at least one other suitor.

On Friday, 4 July Annie worked the late shift and, after arriving home, retired straight to bed. Not until the Saturday afternoon did she rise from her bed, soon after heading to the post office and returning within thirty minutes at approximately 4:30pm. She spoke with her mother who later said she had looked well and in good spirits.

At 9:35pm, some two and a half miles from Gaulby, farmer Joseph Powell discovered her lifeless body lying partly on her back and her left side. She had blood coming from her nose and blood had also pooled beneath her head. When the local constable arrived, he made a thorough search of the area. He noted no sign of a struggle and initially surmised she had come off her bicycle, either through illness or owing to a rut or hole in the road. It should be noted that this part of the lane had two gates. Both would have had to be negotiated in order to reach the spot where she was found. Most interestingly, this route was not the shortest way to her home.

PC Hall returned the next day to conduct a second search. His persistence resulted in the discovery of a bullet, almost buried in the dusty soil and apparently trampled on by the hooves of passing horses. A subsequent examination of the body revealed a bullet wound behind her left ear, with a second wound over the right cheek bone. Small bullets were often overlooked in this era when the most obvious indication of gunshots came in the form of powder burn marks. At the subsequent inquest PC Hall was afforded the highest praise by the Attorney General for his exceptional work in respect of this case.

On the afternoon of 5 July 1919, two young girls were cycling along the road from Leicester when they saw a man cycling in the opposite direction. He smiled and spoke to them as he passed – a pleasant enough greeting and nothing out of the ordinary. Soon afterwards events took on a more sinister turn, indeed quite literally, for not only had he turned and followed them but he very soon overtook them. The eldest, 14-year-old Muriel Mooney and her friend Valeria Caven, a year her junior, both spoke of him asking each to take the lead, but they refused.

Understandably alarmed the girls made a U-turn, riding quickly away and leaving the man standing at a farm gate after he stopped to make some adjustment to his bicycle. This road connected with the one where Miss Wright would be found later that day. When the news of Annie Wright's death came through, the girls, having told their families of the encounter with the stranger, were interviewed by the police and gave a good description, including that he carried a raincoat and that his bicycle was an enamelled green colour.

At 7:30pm Annie Wright arrived at Gaulby, specifically the house of John Measures, her uncle. When she arrived, she was accompanied by a man on a green bicycle who was later seen to be waiting outside by both Mr Measures and Mr and Mrs Evans, Annie's cousins. She stayed for approximately one hour. As she left, the man spoke to her saying, 'Bella, I thought you'd gone the other way.' Riding off together this was the last known sighting of Annie Wright until she was found by the farmer.

For eight months the case baffled police who were unable to find a single lead. Then a boatman travelling along the Grand Union Canal found the tow rope to his horse had fouled on something below the surface. On investigation, he discovered the culprit to be a green bicycle frame. He dropped it back into the water, making a note of where he left it. Next day, 24 February 1920, and now travelling south from Leicester, he retrieved the frame and the still-attached front wheel. With the 'Green Bicycle Mystery' still making the news, he alerted the police who summoned expert help. This enabled them to trace what proved to be a rare bicycle to a buyer a decade earlier in 1910.

Ronald Vivian Light, aged 34, a demobilized army officer, had recently taken the position of mathematics master at a school in Cheltenham. A well-educated man, employed as a draughtsman at the Midland Railway Company in Derby from 1906 to 1914, he returned home to his parents on 2 October that year. Soon after he obtained a commission in the Royal Engineers, although he promptly resigned and enlisted with the Honourable Artillery Company from which he was demobilized in February 1919. Supported by his parents until January 1920, he successfully applied for the position as teacher of mathematics at the Cheltenham school.

During his time in Derby he purchased a BSA (Birmingham Small Arms Company) bicycle in enamelled green from the Orton Brothers bicycle shop in May 1910. Aside from the unusual colour, it had several special fittings. On returning to his parents, Light took the bicycle to a Mr Cox in Leicester for repairs. Having been approached by the police to identify the bicycle, Mr Cox confirmed that this was the machine – ID 103.640 found on the front fork, although the number under the saddle had been filed off.

The repaired bicycle was collected by the family's domestic servant on 5 July, at the request of Light, saying he wished to go for a ride that evening. He was asked to be home by 8pm promptly as a hot supper would be ready for the family, yet it was around 10:30 that evening when he returned saying he had experienced problems with the bicycle. Three or four days later the servant saw Light move his bicycle to the box room at the top of the house where it remained. The servant remarked to police how prior to 5 July he had ridden regularly but since then she had not seen him use it once.

Meanwhile on 12 March, a man named Chambers found the rear wheel of what proved to be the same bicycle. This saw police begin a long search with what was described as a periscope, recovering a revolver and cartridges on 19 March and a match for the bullet was recovered by PC Hall the day after Annie's death. By the time the matching gear wheel, crank, and pedals were found on 29 April, police were able to charge Ronald Light, and for the first time in months the case vanished from the newspapers until it came to court before Justice Horridge.

Unlike the majority of cases, the evidence and witness statements covered a significant area. Hence the judge ordered a detailed map of the area be brought into court beforehand, taking the extraordinary step of leaving the bench and addressing the jury personally, pointing out relevant areas on the map from the side of the jury box. So unusual was such an act by a judge that the press went to some lengths to highlight it in the verbose style of the time. One report said: 'This demographic procedure made an animated court scene, a shaft of sunlight falling from a high casement upon the scarlet robes of the judge, pointing out with his *pince-nez* the roads to the crowd of jurymen in front of him.'

After hearing from the deceased's mother, Mary Wright, and farmer Joseph Powell, who had discovered the body, PC Hall reiterated his role in recovering the bullet. The officer added how, during a search for other evidence, he noted bloody claw marks on a nearby gate, this leading him to find a dead crow which had perched there before succumbing to its own gluttony, gorging on blood.

A Dr Williams provided evidence from the post mortem, bringing to court a fragment of the deceased's skin preserved in a bottle. This had been taken from the area where the bullet had entered. After clarifying a number of medical points, he responded to questioning on where the gunman fired from, stating it was likely to have been half a mile away and it had passed clean through her skull before dropping to the ground.

During Light's time on remand two other witnesses came forward. A second farmer and the wife of a carrier both testified to seeing Miss Wright in the company of a man on a green bike during that last afternoon of her life. Both identified the accused as the man seen.

George Measures, her uncle, repeated his knowledge of events on that fateful day. He also took time to point out that he saw the accused wandering up and down some fifty yards along the road and how he had managed to appear outside almost the instant they all emerged from his house. He thought it odd how, when asked, she told him the man was a complete stranger as he had addressed her as 'Bella', a most familiar mode of address for 1919 and at any time for a supposed stranger.

Another of the guests at the house, son-in-law James Evans, told of speaking to Light outside the house and asking him about his bike. He was told it was a BSA, the then technological marvel of the back-pedalling brake and three-speed gear controlled from the handlebar. Evans noted the unusual colours, the green frame with black mudguards, hearing how the man had spent money on recent repairs to a machine he was clearly proud of owning. Counsel here stressed that the couple had departed at 9:15pm on the friendliest of terms.

Next on the witness stand came Miss Edith Tunnicliffe of Thames Road, Derby. This lady had known Light from 1910 as they had been work colleagues in Derby. Indeed they had kept company on many occasions, and she even visited his mother with him in 1912. They had ridden their bicycles together on a number of occasions, he on a green BSA. After he joined the Army they wrote regularly. In 1916 his letter told her to expect a parcel, although he said she should not open it but simply take it to his parents' home in Leicester. However, she admitted to opening it and found it contained a revolver. She never did understand why Light had sent this. She said she had no knowledge of the search for the man with a green bike until after his arrest when she was contacted by the police.

After hearing evidence from farm labourer John Adams, who witnessed the accused walking alongside the woman cycling in the direction of Gaulby, a Leicester gunsmith's testimony on the gun and bullets and evidence proving the manufacturer, buyer and seller of the bicycle, Muriel Webb gave evidence. Employed as the domestic servant for some years, Miss Webb added that she had only seen the bicycle on one further occasion after early July. This was around Christmas time when the accused brought it down from the box room well after dark, took it straight out and she never saw it again.

When called to give evidence Light first spoke of his time in the Army. He bought a Webley & Scott service revolver from a Major Benton in July 1915, taking it with him to France in November of the following year. He could not recall what he had in mind when he sent it to Miss Tunnicliffe, but had done so when he discovered that it could not be secured in the bag of his motorcycle. He returned to Britain in August 1918 suffering from shell shock and deafness, and he had continued hearing problems. He agreed that both the bicycle and the holster had been his, but had no notion of how these came to be found in the canal and he had not seen them for ages until shown to him by the police.

His version of events on 5 July began with a visit to see some friends of his mother at Oadby. He cycled there along the main road to Great Glen and Little Stretton, but denied meeting the two girls then or on the return journey. Arriving back at Little Stretton he noted the time and, wanting to arrive home between 8pm and 8:30pm, he opted for a longer route and met up with a young woman examining her bicycle. Although he had never seen her before, he offered a helping hand and thought the problem may have been due to excessive play on the front wheel but he did not have the tools to fix it.

Together they rode downhill and walked together up the hills as she was off to see friends at Gaulby, a place he did not know. Leaving her at her friend's house, he waited a few minutes before cycling up to the church where he noticed a puncture which he repaired. By the time he finished it was 8:15pm and, riding back along the road, he saw the same girl who said, 'You've been a long time.' He denied calling her by name, saying he did not know it until much later after reading the account in the paper.

Together they rode in the general direction of home but he had recurring problems with his tyre, which forced him to stop regularly and pump it back up. At this time, she commented that her tyres would never get into such a sorry state as she worked for a tyre factory, which meant she could get them at cost price. He pointed out that his bicycle had not been ridden for a while, hence the problem. They parted ten minutes later and he made straight for Leicester saying he would doubtless have to stop and pump up the tyre several times on the journey, which indeed he did before arriving home at 10pm.

It was Tuesday when he first read about the case and admitted he should have come forward at that time. He also said he did slacken bolts and nuts on the bike and throw it into the canal and, once again, he could now see that this had been foolhardy and he apologized for allowing the police to follow a false trail for so long.

The jury retired at 5pm and returned three hours later with their verdict of not guilty. Both inside and outside the court the announcement was met with wild applause. A century on and the real killer, assuming the verdict was the right one, has never been found.

After his trial, Light vanished from public life, although now we know he was living at Leysdown-on-Sea on the Isle of Sheppey in 1928 as Leonard Estelle. Six years later he married Lilian Lester, widow of Sergeant Ernest Lester who was killed in action in 1917 and who also served with the Royal Engineers. The widow abandoned her two sons at a Wolverhampton orphanage with her youngest, a daughter, remaining in her care. Only when Light died in 1975, aged 89, did his stepdaughter learn about the trial fifty-five years earlier.

Two books have been written investigating the case. In 1930 *The Green Bicycle Case* by H. R. Wakefield suggested that the verdict was the right one, while C. Wendy East's *The Green Bicycle Murder* in 1993 tries to convince us the killer got away.

In later years there came the suggestion of the right man being arrested but that he should never have been charged for it was an accident. Levi Bowley, a Leicester superintendent, is said to have obtained a confession by Light while awaiting trial, which claimed the gun went off while Light cleaned it. That this note never came to court as evidence seems sufficient to show this story has been concocted well after the event and thus can be discarded.

Yet other evidence still exists. Both the holster and cartridges, seven of them blanks, were purchased by an anonymous collector in America for $6,000 at a 1987 auction at Christie's. Most macabrely, the bicycle hung on the wall of a bike shop in Evington for several decades but disappeared some years ago and its current location is unknown.

Chapter 39

1921 Mary Sutcliffe

Today the Leeds and Liverpool Canal continues to challenge boat owners as they negotiate ninety-one locks over its 127-mile length. Near the eastern end is the entrance to the Bradford Canal, with ten locks over its three-and-a-half miles. Opening in 1774, it closed in 1882 for four years when it was considered a health hazard, before closing permanently in 1922.

Initially as part of Bradford's bid to be European Capital of Culture in 2008, reopening the canal had been a very real possibility. Seen as the catalyst for regeneration and capitalizing on this as the boom leisure industry, two-thirds of the route is already owned by the council. Visitors walking the route today may find it difficult to visualize just where the canal fitted into the landscape. Names such as Wharf Street and Canal Road offer clues but perhaps the best reminder can be seen when, having descended the very steep route of the aptly-named Prospect Road, it offers good views over the valley below.

As Prospect Road ends, at least for motor vehicles, heading off north is Spinkwell Close. This name was taken from the former Spink Well Lock and, with the close to one's back, the drop from the upper level is quite obvious on the opposite side. Look to your right and, having sat here for almost a century, we find the massive dressed stones once used to line the canal bank and still in a rough line across what passes for an early idea of landscaping.

Having found the line of the canal, imagine the towpath where boats passed through the lock gates. This crime dates from the year before the canal's closure, although clearly at the time it was still operational as the lock-keeper is in residence and a major witness to events.

It was never clear how 43-year-old Charles Grimshaw and 35-year-old Mary Sutcliffe became acquainted. Motor mechanic Grimshaw's official residence of Mountford Street, Sparkhill in Birmingham had little to connect him with the Sutcliffe household in Bolton Woods, Bradford. Yet this was by no means the first time Grimshaw lodged at 47 Fletcher Lane and thus the man and woman clearly knew each other and, as it transpired, did so intimately.

In November 1921, the story unfolded in the courtroom as to events of the first Tuesday of October. The accused and the victim walked along the towpath heading for the Sutcliffe's home, having spent the afternoon and early evening together after meeting in Bradford. For reasons unclear, as they walked along Grimshaw attacked the woman with a razor. In her statement Mary Sutcliffe told how, on seeing the blood, he had cried out: 'Good God, I have cut your throat. I am going to finish you outright!'

Mary managed to wrest the weapon from him and, throwing it down, ran to the cottage of the lock-keeper just ninety yards away. Here both the lock-keeper and his son heard the man's one-word reply of, 'Jealousy!' when Sutcliffe asked why he had done it. When the police arrived they found Grimshaw sitting at the side of the canal, head in hands, clearly upset and with the blood-stained razor mere feet away. He had not resisted arrest and cooperated while in custody.

Cross-examined by the prosecution counsel, Grimshaw maintained he had no recollection of why he had a razor in his hand or how he had injured her. Responding to the suggestion he had not had sufficient to drink to affect his memory, the prisoner pointed out he had not eaten that day and that he had also suffered from head injuries incurred during his time as a professional boxer. He also added that he and Mary Sutcliffe had never had a quarrel and were always on 'affectionate' terms.

Of more interest are the prisoner's responses when the prosecution's questioning turned to his relationship with Mary Sutcliffe. Under the counsel's questioning, Grimshaw did not deny that they had been on the most of intimate terms but refuted suggestions he had wanted to continue their acquaintance. His guilt unquestioned, the judge pointed out that such a 'short and sordid story' could easily have resulted in a charge of murder. Justice Salter remarked on his previous good character and sentenced him to just twelve months' imprisonment.

The case may have been settled in the eyes of the law but, approaching a century later, more questions are raised than answered. It seems both parties claimed their relationship had ended and yet, if so, why did Grimshaw travel up to Bradford that Tuesday morning and why had Mary Sutcliffe arranged to meet him? If the meeting had been for the most part amicable (remember they had spent the afternoon and part of the evening together) what happened on the canal bank – or just before – to change the mood? Twelve months does seem a laughably short sentence while the prosecution's cross-examination of the victim could be said to show that she was not entirely blameless.

However it is the one person we never hear from who proves the most intriguing. What of Mr Sutcliffe? From the report of the trial it is clear he was present and undoubtedly aware of his wife's affair with their former lodger. So, what role did he play and why was he not called to give evidence?

With all the figures in the case long gone these questions will never be answered.

Chapter 40

1926 William Mulvanny

Perhaps not every perpetrator of a crime should be classified a criminal. In the post-war years of the 1920s times were hard for many. These were times of great change and across the globe economies were in varying degrees of recession. Jobs were not safe but still families had to be supported.

One man trying to keep his family warm and food in their bellies was William Mulvanny. An unemployed collier, he was found stealing coal from a railway siding running parallel to the canal in St Helens. The arresting police officer made Mulvanny carry the evidence on his back to the police station, thus greatly reducing the chances of him escaping.

What the police constable could never have envisaged was Mulvanny slipping from his grasp and diving into the canal while still holding the sack of coal. Quickly losing sight of the man, the constable who was unable to swim, went for assistance. Unfortunately, on their return they were only in time to drag the lifeless body from the canal. At the inquest, the coroner returned a verdict of misadventure.

Yet the case did not end there as the coroner, Mr Brighouse, turned his attention to the widow Mulvanny. He asked how she and her four young children had coped since the sad loss of her husband. She replied how, in the six weeks since his death, the parish assistance and unemployment benefit they had previously relied upon had stopped. Since then she had been forced to sell everything she owned simply to feed the children. A table and one bed on which all five slept was all they had left.

The coroner pointed out that this had been the most drastic punishment for a man who was simply trying to honour his responsibilities. While what he did was wrong, there had been no malice in his actions and this was merely the response of a desperate man in desperate times.

Tellingly the coroner added, 'One half of the world doesn't know how the other half lives.' He then made a grant of £5 from his own funds, stipulating but one condition: that she should spend the money wisely and not on an expensive funeral for her late husband. 'Bury him decently but most economically,' he said. 'Then spend the rest of the money on yourself and your children.'

Chapter 41

1927 The Bushells

On the Birmingham and Fazeley Canal in September 1927, a keen-eyed policeman spotted some suspicious happenings at Minworth. A boat belonging to John F. Cox of Bordesley Green in Birmingham had moored up and, as the policeman watched, an estimated ninety pounds of coal was unloaded and dropped over a fence into a garden.

Police Constable Robinson went to the boat in order to question the men about their actions. However the four men obstructed the officer in his duty, pushing him away and not allowing him near the boat or the coal. Summoning help, it took several officers to bring the four men to Coleshill Police Station.

On Friday, 10 September, four men were brought before Coleshill Magistrates. Stephen Bushell and John Wilfrid Bushell of Westley Street, Bordesley, Birmingham were both charged with stealing the coal, while Henry Bushell and Frank Edgar Bushell of Pitt Street, Birmingham were charged with obstructing the police in the execution of their duty.

Despite the apparent severity of the offences – stealing almost a hundredweight of coal and manhandling an officer of the law – the magistrates saw fit to dispense almost laughably minimal punishments. Both Stephen and John Bushell, who had been charged with theft, were bound over to keep the peace and ordered to pay £1 13s 6d costs each. While those who effectively assaulted PC Robinson, Henry and Frank Bushell, received fines of £2 and £1 respectively.

Chapter 42

1927 Olive Turner

Inner-city redevelopment programmes have made the canalside prime sites for modern leisure and residential properties. Add in how canals have proved to be *the* boom leisure industry and it is clear why the second city would want to promote itself as 'having more miles of canal than Venice'. Of course the two are very different in size and thus the twenty-six miles in Venice is in such a small area it would be very difficult to hide a crime, as indeed it proved in Birmingham's thirty-six miles of inner-city canal and 174 miles including the surrounding area.

Even with all those miles of towpath in Birmingham, and with the heyday of the canal network long gone, could night hide the events of the evening of 2 July 1927? All was revealed when the case eventually came before Lord Ilkeston at Birmingham Assizes on Friday, 9 December 1927. James Joseph Power aged 33, a former policeman, was charged with the murder of 18-year-old Olive Gordon Turner and for demanding money with menaces.

After the usual court formalities, the case for the prosecution began with evidence from Dr John Cathies of Lodge Road who had examined the body. He spoke of the woman being dragged from the canal on the Wednesday morning, after her bag, fur and hat had been found the previous evening. He first examined the body on the canal bank before conducting the post mortem.

Water had been present in the lungs, making the official cause of death drowning although there were other factors to be taken into consideration. No water in the stomach indicated the lack of a swallow reflex and thus she was unconscious when she entered the water, and the only external sign of injury was significant bruising to the left side of her forehead. In his opinion, this would have knocked the girl out and all indications were this had not happened when she was in the water but before she entered it.

Next her sister spoke of the deceased. Ivy Gordon Turner had last seen her sister on the evening of 2 July when she left their home at 7:30pm. She was stepping out with Charles Broomhead, her sweetheart, and at that time she was in good health and good spirits, with no marks on her. On being asked to identify her sister's watch she was quite distressed and, with no further evidence to offer, the judge excused her.

Eyewitness Thomas Hill of Winson Green spoke of passing by this arm of the canal at Lodge Road at around 7:40pm. He noted three people: a woman, whom he identified from a photograph as the victim, and two men. The larger man, this the prisoner, obscured his view of the smaller man, hence he could not identify this as Charles Broomhead. He heard Power demanding money but the couple refused, at which the larger man became angered and, with his arm firmly around the victim's waist, led her away along the towpath. She was never seen alive again.

When Charles Broomhead came to the witness stand he said Power had identified himself as a policeman. Charles replied that he had always had great respect for the police and so did not intervene when Olive was marched away but, on reflection, thought the actions were not what he would expect of an officer of the law. It had later been Charles – who recognized Power when leaving his place of work and realized he was clearly not a policeman – who had sent for the police leading to his arrest.

When the prosecution made the court aware other witnesses had also identified Power from a line-up at the police station, the prisoner laughed out loud. The judge ordered him to be silent. Power mumbled a reply and, when asked to repeat it so the court could hear, he accused the witnesses of lying, saying he knew the police were not above paying supposed witnesses to give evidence leading to a conviction.

Other witnesses helped to build up a picture of events that evening. A woman saw a man climb a wall alongside the canal and gain access to an entry leading into the street. She thought the prisoner could have been that man but could not be certain. Frank Pritchett lived in Brookfield Road and, as he made his way to bed that evening, had heard 'a horrifying scream, as of a woman in fright'. One Mrs Florence Robinson also heard the awful scream.

The arresting detective spoke next. Having spoken to Charles Broomhead at the police station he made his way to the factory and took Power into custody. When the defence counsel suggested the police had been looking for a suspect wearing a light grey suit, the detective denied any colour clothing had been mentioned. At this point Power leapt up and called the witness a liar and, once more, the judge ordered him to be quiet.

For the first time the public then heard of an almost identical event earlier that year. On 3 August, while on remand, Power had been charged with what was described as 'an offence against a woman' on 23 May and of also assaulting a man at 11pm that same night. The couple had joined the canal at Winson Green, whereupon a man (identified as Power) approached menacingly saying he was a police officer. A struggle ensued and the accused was said to have knocked him down with so hard a blow that not only did he have a cut lip but he remained unsteady on his feet for a good two hours thereafter.

Understandably the woman attempted to flee but Power easily restrained her. Holding her firmly by the arm he led her away, she assumed to Dudley Road Police Station. Instead they stopped beneath a canal bridge, whereupon she said he was no policeman and while he claimed to hold a card she did not see any proof. Following the assault, the terrified woman had made her way home, and hadn't reported the incident until 7 July after hearing of the similarity of the attack leading to the murder. She had not screamed out during the attack, as she feared she would be knocked about had she done so but ever since she had been petrified and often in a stupor. She admitted that had it not been for the murder charge she would not have reported the assault. Neither she nor the man wished to be named as she wanted to keep her good name and blot out the awful memory.

After summing up, the judge asked the jury to retire to consider their verdict. They debated for just one hour before finding James Joseph Power guilty of murder. Turning to Power, the judge asked if he wanted to say anything before passing sentence. Power spoke slowly and clearly, informing the jury and witnesses that they had made an honest mistake. Indeed, were it not for the evidence of a certain detective inspector he would be walking free. He claimed the man had had it in for him ever since he left the police force.

Power also spoke at length of a visit from the same detective just a month prior to the trial, where he made him aware of further evidence in the form of the anonymous woman's allegation. Although never saying so, he hinted that the second woman's accusations had been falsified by the detective and the woman. He then went on to describe how the detective had picked up a poker, attempting to provoke Power into attacking him saying, 'Come on, I'll smash your brains in' and insisting that both the prison governor and several wardens had witnessed the same.

When Lord Ilkeston sentenced Power to death, he responded by saying he would appeal and that the jury had sent yet another innocent man to the gallows. His appeal, both heard and rejected on 13 January 1928, was based on the lack of proof he had ever been on the canal, something he had strongly denied since his arrest. He also asked, if the police were convinced of his guilt, why had it been necessary for a second version to be brought up months later? He also pointed out that the woman had never made a complaint and, as he had never known her identity, he could not be expected to defend himself.

A crowd gathered outside Winson Green Prison in Birmingham early on the morning of Tuesday, 31 January 1928. Most of the several hundred present were women. Public hangings had been abolished in the 1860s, thus all they saw was the official emerging to announce the sentence had been carried out at 8am that morning and that the murderer was dead.

Chapter 43

1931 The Preston Hundreds

It is rare to find clearly defined lines in law. One has precedents set and subsequently followed in the courtroom, but what of the role of the police? How far can the police go in deciding when to prosecute, to give a warning or even turn a blind eye? Such will have been asked many times in Preston in the first week of February 1931 when just ten individuals were called to account for their actions.

In court, the defendants were instructed to line up as the dock proved far too small to accommodate so many. All were charged with stealing coal, amounting to at least ten hundredweight, which was the property of the London, Midland and Scottish (LMS) Railway Company. Each entered a plea individually, although something of a farce ensued when the court instantly dismissed the charges against two of the ten. One man was discovered to be totally deaf, unable to read or write or hold a conversation, while a second who answered to the name read out was found to be the wife of the accused who was also dismissed.

Within minutes of the case coming into the courtroom, all control was lost. Many comments were overheard – from the gallery as well as the dock – all questioning how, when every suspect had been covered in the filth of the canal and the coal, could anyone be identified as having been among those who had gone into the now empty canal to help themselves. The response, hardly what we would expect from a sombre courtroom, was: 'There were a hundred and more of you, all dirty, and while it was raining, dirt does not descend from the heavens.' The suggestion being the filth which coated them from head to foot was surely sufficient proof of their guilt.

When normality returned, Mr J. C. Philips of the LMS legal department set out the case against the remaining eight men, all of whom hailed from Preston. On Saturday, 10 January, a stretch of the Lancaster Canal had burst about one-and-a-quarter-miles from Preston. Within a short time literally hundreds had descended on the now empty canal to help themselves to the coal exposed on the bottom. Over the years this had built up and a reasonable amount littered the area, having been spilled when loading or simply while manoeuvring.

It had been impossible to count or dispel the huge numbers. A number of different containers were carried here, including handcarts, barrows, buckets, trucks, even baskets or pots, anything they could lay their hands on. Not content with what could be found in the mud of the canal, others climbed on to the trucks in the adjacent railway siding and began throwing more coal down into the empty canal.

When the Railway Police arrived at around 5pm they began taking names. Those questioned were thought to account for approximately ten hundredweight of coal, although it was estimated perhaps two-and-a-half times that amount had been removed that day – much of which had never seen the bottom of the canal before it had burst that day. Constable Yardley of the Railway Police reported how the fading light at the time of their arrival made it difficult to identify anyone, especially as they were all utterly filthy. Hence they satisfied themselves with taking the names of those willing to give them.

At this point the trial took on a more frivolous tone. Defence counsel, Mr Ashton, pointed out that coal falling in the street could be collected by anyone and would never be regarded as stealing. Thus, how could coal dropped into the canal be seen as any different? He encouraged one defendant to relate how, when the level of the water dropped, it had been common practice ever since the canal had been opened to help clear the bottom of the coal. Indeed, the people should be applauded for their 'jolly hard work' as collection often meant standing in frigid water up to the ears and, in his opinion, they fully deserved the small quantity of coal gathered.

Another defendant, a Mr Maloney, said he had no charge to answer. On the day in question he had gone to the canal to find his children. When he saw what was happening he took it upon himself to chase a number of other children off and, when he was stopped by police at the gate, his bag of coal had been what he had managed to retrieve from the fleeing children.

In closing Mr Phillips spoke of how the coal in the canal could never be considered 'lost' as it would in the street, for the canal belonged to the company, as did the wagons, the siding, and the boats. He also spoke at length about the huge amount of missing coal, some of which undoubtedly came from the wagons in the siding. He conceded that some of the coal would have fallen into the canal over the years but there could be no doubt that a great deal of 'lost' coal retrieved from the canal that day had not fallen but had been pushed.

Magistrates had no chance in coming to a decision which Mr Phillips and the LMS Company would consider satisfactory. Just eight remaining persons were in court to answer the charges and, as the police had confirmed, there had been more than 100 involved when they arrived, many of whom were children. The bench was aware of the long custom of obtaining coal from the canal in this way, yet this did not make it right. Dismissing the accused under the Probation of Offenders Act, they warned that any repeat actions would be considered theft and dealt with accordingly.

Chapter 44

1936 Eliza Worton

Walking along the canal at 8:10am near Gospel Oak Bridge, Tipton on the morning of 15 February 1936, canal ganger John Evans spotted something beneath the iced-over surface. Looking closer he saw it was a woman and he immediately broke the ice and dragged her body to the side. As he feared, she was quite cold and quite dead.

So began the trial of 36-year-old lorry driver William Frederick Oakley of Bilston Street, Sedgley who was charged with the murder of Eliza Jane Worton aged 25 of Phoenix Street, West Bromwich. Evans went on to explain that he sought assistance and, having given his details to the police officer, allowed them to continue their investigation.

PC Johnson then took up the tale as he had attended the scene when summoned by the previous witness. He described the deceased as having hair matted with blood, this from many head wounds, with another very obvious wound on the bridge of her nose. He examined the area and found no sign of a struggle or of footmarks, which he might have expected to find set into the frozen ground.

Medical evidence showed her death had been from drowning, although it was undoubtedly hastened by the icy water. Wounds to her head, although a contributory factor, had not been the cause but indicated that death had come quickly after she entered the water. That the blood had seeped slowly from the wounds and had not dissipated by the victim thrashing for her life in the water showed the heart had stopped quickly.

An unnamed 16-year-old boy pointed out blood stains on the road across Gospel Oak Bridge to the police. Two other boys came forward to speak of a lorry parked on the bridge the previous night. Surprisingly observant boys, they recalled the name on the side as 'Oakley, Upper Ettingshall, Coseley' and how a rear light had been faulty. A bystander told of how, on hearing a lorry door slam, he looked across to see the driver get down from the cab and follow the first person, whom he assumed had been the one to slam the door, but he could not see either individual clearly enough to identify them. However, they did both say the driver wore 'a shiny peaked cap'. The boys added that they saw the lorry drive away shortly afterwards.

Tracing Oakley from his van, he reported to Bilston Police Station on the evening of 15 February accompanied by his brother. Here they observed him scraping blood from his clothing with a pen knife and also noted blood on the angle bracket of the lorry. This must have been fresh blood for, unlike the rest of the vehicle, it was not covered by dust.

During questioning Oakley's story changed. Initially the police interview of Oakley had suggested this was a hit and run accident. Oakley replied that he would know if he had run someone over, he was a good driver and should he ever hit anyone he would immediately give up driving and if they disbelieved him just look at his lorry. When they pointed out fresh blood had been found on his vehicle he claimed he had no knowledge of how it got there.

Oakley also denied being on the bridge that night and denied ever going that way. Furthermore, he had returned to his garage by 9:50pm on 14 February and had been alone with his vehicle since 5:30pm. A problem with the lorry meant he had to unload the bricks and make repairs before reloading, thus it took more than four hours to reach his home address.

Oakley was retained overnight and the following day his story began to show inconsistencies. He had originally denied knowing the woman, although he had known of her disappearance saying he had been asked by her aunt, Mrs Robbins, 'What have you done with our Jennie?' with Mr Robbins adding, 'I should not be surprised if they found her in the cut.' Later that same day he changed his mind and admitted he had seen Mrs Worton at her place of work at 2pm on Friday 14 February, then he retracted that and said he had not seen her since the Friday morning.

The case against him was mounting when a witness identified his vehicle in Phoenix Street – home to Mrs Worton – at the very time Oakley claimed he had been at home. Forensics were still unheard of but the rudimentary science of the time showed the blood on the bridge was group three, the same as the deceased. It had not been possible to identify the blood stains on Oakley's clothing, nor on the lorry.

Charged with the murder of Eliza Jane Worton, he appeared in court and listened as the evidence against him grew. When defence counsel

Norman Birkett QC began he asked why Mrs Worton's husband never featured at any time in this case. At this point it was revealed that the sailor had left the family home in July 1834, had not been seen since and was undoubtedly unaware he was a widower.

Mr Birkett continued, suggesting that Mrs Worton would have been lonely after such a time and, while telling her parents she was visiting the Labour Exchange (employment office) on that Friday evening, she had never arrived and was it not unusual for an employed woman to look for work? He was clearly intimating Eliza Worton had arranged a secret liaison on the night of her death.

Turning to the main prosecution witnesses, the two unusually observant boys, Mr Birkett asked how much of their vital evidence could be trusted. He recalled every scrap of their evidence: the name and address on the side of the lorry, the faulty rear light on a stationary vehicle, which was presumably not lit, and how the driver got out of the cab wearing a 'shiny peaked cap'. At this point he produced Oakley's headwear, a flat cap seen as greasy or dirty but certainly not 'shiny'.

With a lack of motive, no evidence of a quarrel, and no proof the two had been together near the bridge on that evening or any other time Oakley was acquitted. The circumstances surrounding Eliza Worton's death remain an unsolved mystery.

Chapter 45

1939 Edith Vincent

When it comes to the canal network the focus is always on the Midlands, with arteries in the general direction of the capital and to Cheshire with its salt and the cotton mills of Lancashire. Yet there were canals in many other parts of the country, some which are still in use. One of these is at Exeter in Devon where, in the summer months of 1939, a murder victim was discovered.

At around 7pm on Saturday, 24 June, a young lad named Peter Squire wandered into the Great Marsh Field and, on the banks of the Exeter Canal, saw a woman lying face down near the bushes. She had a coat over her back and her feet were bare. He had been very scared and ran away.

While not reporting it, he did mention it to his friends next day and, not believing him, they had gone to investigate. Thus the official discovery of the body came that following day. At 3pm Dennis Wilton and some friends were walking the towpath when they saw the younger boys gathered round something, joined them and saw it was a woman. Realizing she was dead he immediately telephoned the police.

Fifteen minutes later PC Palmer arrived to find a woman lying face down with a tweed overcoat covering her from the waist to the knees. Removing the coat, he discovered the green cardigan and red dress she wore were torn, leaving her naked from the hem of the cardigan to the top of her stockings. Turning the body over he found her vest and dress torn, leaving her naked from the neck down. Between her knees she gripped a torn fragment of red material, which was from her dress, while to one side were her left shoe, her corset and her smalls. A little over a yard away he found her right shoe, felt hat, and what was later described as an American leather shopping bag. He then discovered another scrap of red material on a bush and piece of a brooch.

Sending for a Dr Gray, photographs were taken and an initial examination of the body made. He noted bloodstained fluid from her mouth and blood from her right ear. At the subsequent post mortem, performed by Drs Ross and Webster, a bruise above her left eyebrow, seemingly from being struck with a fist, and other bruising across the area of her chin, throat and to the nose were all indicative of an assault by a powerful individual. A number of tiny scratches on her face were clearly caused by her lying face down as these were from the prickles on the bush.

Internally the doctors discovered bruises on either side of the larynx, itself damaged and filled with blood. The hyoid, a horseshoe-shaped bone in the neck, had been fractured with one end broken off. To the left temple a deep-seated bruise showed further evidence of a beating, while the many pinpoint haemorrhages found internally were clear evidence that the cause of death was asphyxia. She had been strangled.

Identified as Mrs Edith Mabel Vincent of 111 Foxhayes Road, Exeter, she left home at 7:20am on the Friday morning heading for her workplace at Exeter Laundries. Friday was pay day and, as always on pay day, she carried her American leather shopping bag and her handbag. She was also wearing the wedding ring her husband had purchased just four months earlier. After working until 5pm she then collected her wages of £1 5s 10d, before heading for the New Golden Lion public house in Market Street where witnesses saw her in conversation with a man.

That man was later identified as William George Witherington, a 34-year-old labourer of 34 Wrights Avenue, Torquay. Currently unemployed, Witherington lived with his two boys, aged 8 and 6, and his 5-year-old daughter. His wife, who had been diagnosed with cancer, had been hospitalized. Despite living in Torquay, Witherington was no stranger to Exeter, or indeed to the New Golden Lion. He was seen there that Friday lunchtime only hours after signing on at Torquay and a day after collecting unemployment assistance of £1 15s 6d, when he was rather generously buying drinks for others as well as himself.

By 4pm on Friday, funds seemingly exhausted, Witherington arrived at the unemployment offices in Exeter looking for help. Staff asked if he could account for the monies received the previous day in Torquay, whereupon he listed spending well in excess of the money paid to him. Correctly thinking the money had been spent on drink they eventually gave him 3s 6d, which was sufficient only for his fare home, but he became abusive and demanded more. Police officers were eventually called to remove him and although he did return, he was now much calmer, and appeared satisfied when told to report to the Torquay office on Monday morning. Yet he did not return to Torquay but to the inn, and there he was seen talking to Mrs Vincent.

They remained there until approximately 9:30pm when, walking via Fore Street, they were seen by Mrs Rundle at the Devonport Inn where they stayed until shortly after 10pm. Mrs Vincent was known to Mrs Rundle, as was her prized American leather shopping bag. That evening she was seen handling a ten shilling note and a good amount of silver but when her body was discovered she had no money, no handbag, and no new wedding ring.

A little over an hour later a porter named Thorn cycled along the quay, this being the opposite bank of the canal from Great Marsh Fields. In the still of the night he heard a woman scream. Such was the terror in the scream he stopped to listen. Straining to pick up any sound he waited for several minutes but heard nothing. He admitted the scream had been enough to frighten him and he had cycled away rather relieved that he had not felt obliged to investigate further.

The next sighting of Witherington came shortly after midnight at Peamore Garage, approximately four miles from Exeter's city centre. Entering the garage café, he ordered food and witnesses overheard him speaking of having walked from Exeter and of the row at the unemployment offices on the Friday. He remained there much of the night, talking at length with a lorry driver named Bolwell, and the two left at 5am, with Witherington being offered a ride as far as Newton Abbott. Shortly before 8am he was spotted by a neighbour, Mrs Knapman, walking along Wrights Avenue towards his home.

On Sunday, 25 June, a friend named Godbeer met with Witherington, telling him of work available in Yeovil, presumably cash in hand, but that he would have to fund his own travel. Godbeer understood Witherington would be raising the cash through something he had at home and on Monday he told him he would be pawning his wife's wedding ring. Together they went to the antique shop on Union Street, Torquay belonging to Mr Scudamore, who allowed 4s 2d but Witherington was given 5s. Later it emerged that this had been the wedding ring bought by Mr Vincent for his wife, while the nine-carat ring purchased by Witherington had found its way to a different pawn shop in the same street in July the previous year.

On his way to meet Godbeer, two officers saw him on the seafront at Teignmouth. From here he was taken to Exeter Police Station, where he made and signed his statement and thereafter he was held while his story could be corroborated. This included checking the details on the pawned ring which, unknown to Witherington, was retrieved earlier that day and had been left with him in the interview room on Tuesday, 27 June. Ten minutes later the officer returned to the interview room and the accused broke into floods of tears.

Here Witherington, as the police had hoped, changed his statement – to be accurate he added to his statement. At 10pm that evening Witherington listened as the charge of the murder of Edith Mabel Vincent was read out using the official required wording and resulting in the record of Witherington's reply – 'I did not kill her. I had no intention of killing her, and when I left her she was alive. She said to me, "We won't have any more arguing, give me five shillings instead of ten shillings." I then left her up against a tree where she fell.'

By the time of his trial in November, this earlier evidence had been added to. Doctors, who had already come to the conclusion that she had been strangled, added that the deceased had recently had intercourse. Predictably, prosecution counsel pointed to the response from Witherington when charged and while never referred to specifically, this talk of money could only have been in exchange for intercourse. Additionally, at the time of his arrest the prisoner's description told of him having been scratched quite recently.

At this point spare a thought for her husband listening to the prosecution pointing out how she had prostituted herself that evening. George Frederick Vincent, a boot and shoe repairer of Exwick Road, Foxhayes, Exeter, had been married to Edith for ten years. Together they had six children, sons and daughters now reliant on one parent. He had little to add to proceedings, unlike widow Violet Midson who had known the deceased for a number of years. Coincidentally Mrs Midson had also witnessed the prisoner's aggression at the unemployment exchange for she had been working there as a cleaner. Not only did she see him on that June afternoon when being removed by the police but she had also seen both of them later that evening in the New Golden Lion.

On taking the stand Witherington's barely concealed distress was evident to all as it was announced that, since the arrest, his wife had succumbed to her illness and died on 27 August in a Torquay hospital. Upon his arrest, the authorities had successfully applied for an order allowing the children to be admitted to a Newton Abbott home.

Initially the couple worked together in London. They had pretended to be married by wearing a cheap, ill-fitting wedding ring in order to get the job. Twelve months later they married in Poole, Dorset on 6 February 1937. A year later they moved to Torquay and his wife was diagnosed with cancer shortly afterwards, since when she had been in and out of hospitals and nursing homes.

In order to support his family Witherington had been working in Yeovil. However, he had to return to Torquay after receiving the message of his wife's illness. Initially he took on odd gardening jobs while awaiting news from the assistance department in Exeter. He went on to tell the jury of his journey to Exeter, the argument he had had there, and how he had met Mrs Vincent in the back room of the New Golden Lion around 7:15pm on Friday, 23 June. They were introduced by a woman he knew only as Lizzie and, as the evening progressed, each drank two pints of bottled beer.

Witherington also spoke of a man seated on the other side of Mrs Vincent. He had spoken to them both and asked if they would have a drink with him. Described as 5ft 9 or 10, wearing a trilby and a mackintosh, he thought someone had referred to him as 'Jim' but could not be sure. However, he was sure 'Jim' had spoken of working on the boats on the canal and when he mentioned that he had also worked on boats but at sea, 'Jim' had mumbled a response and carried on talking to the women.

After hearing Mrs Vincent tell 'Jim' later that evening, 'Don't be a mug,' she had asked if he would accompany her to the Devonshire Inn. Here they went into the back room occupied by sixty or seventy people and shared more bottled beer (this making a total of six or seven sixpenny ales) before Mrs Vincent bought a bottle of beer and, after placing it in her shopping bag, they left the premises. As they walked through the passage they saw 'Jim' again, with Mrs Vincent's 'Goodnight' answered by 'Goodnight Eve'.

Together they bought some chips, eating them as they walked down Fore Street, along the bank, across a bridge to the canal basin near the lock-keeper's cottage. They lay on the grass to finish the meal and Witherington noticed a dredger with its lights on near the lock gates. While embracing they had rolled down the grassy bank, stopping at the bottom with a bump. He had no knowledge of how her clothing had been ripped, indeed shortly afterwards, following a disagreement about money, he had picked up a charm, a ring, half a crown and some coppers, all of which had fallen from his pocket, told her he was not satisfied and turned away.

Mrs Vincent had asked him to stay, saying they would just be friends but he said he was going home. All was fine when he left her – she replaced her shoes and he counted the clock striking 11pm. He had no idea she was married and at no time did he notice her wearing a wedding ring, nor did he take money or anything else from her. When asked about his supposed statement of throwing the bag in the canal, as stated by an earlier witness, he denied any knowledge of the bag or its contents. He then told the court how he walked across the suspension bridge, Topsham Road, Countess Weir, arriving at Peamore Garage and received a lift to Newton Abbott, which took him home.

The judge's summing up took an hour and twenty minutes. He pointed out the only real evidence was that they had spent the evening together until the time of the scream or shortly before. The wedding ring, identified by Mr Vincent as belonging to his wife, was a plain band and much the same as many others. In the words of the judge: 'There is no proof it isn't Mrs Vincent's and no proof it isn't Mrs Witherington's ring or that belonging to anyone else.'

The jury retired for a total of ninety minutes. A brief break saw them request another look at the photographs taken at the scene. When they returned they found him not guilty of murder and not guilty of manslaughter. William George Witherington was acquitted and to date nobody else has been brought to trial for her murder.

Chapter 46

1949 Pearl Cowman

Pearl Cowman of Stalybridge was just 13 years of age in 1949. For the last nine years, following the death of her mother, she had lived at her grandmother's home in Henry Street. On 24 August 1949 at 10pm, she received a half crown (2s 6d) from her grandmother and was sent on an unknown errand. Her grandmother did not see her again until she identified the body pulled from the Manchester to Huddersfield Canal two days later.

Meanwhile, shortly after 10:05pm on 24 August, 41-year-old cotton worker Henry Taylor left the Oddfellows Arms, the latest of a number of public houses he visited that night. Almost at the same time Lucy Brent saw her friend Pearl skipping along High Street outside the Oddfellows, where she must have met up with Taylor for another witness, a Mrs Gibbons who knew Taylor well, saw him talking to a young girl answering Pearl's description. They were under the light of a street lamp near the local fish and chip shop. After a brief conversation, both turned along a street in the general direction of the canal.

After the discovery and identification of the body, police launched a hunt for the killer. A post mortem revealed the cause of death as drowning. At the time of death, the position of her tongue and facial muscles suggested a great deal of force had been applied to the nape of the neck but it was insufficient to show strangulation as the cause. She was wearing a bathing suit, the one she was seen wearing earlier that day while paddling in the canal. Her corpse exhibited marks consistent with an assault of a sexual nature, while the bathing suit she still wore had been cut open.

Taylor was arrested while at work on 1 September. His colleague, Alice Roberts, worked opposite him on the same machine. She told police how Taylor had appeared unusually troubled, even distressed, for the past few days. Later, now aware of the charge against him, she reflected on how many of his comments could be seen as admission of guilt.

During initial questioning Taylor, while admitting he knew Pearl, insisted he had not seen her for more than three weeks. Unknown to Taylor, police had interviewed Pearl's friend, Betsy Ann Smith, who said she had gone with Pearl to see Taylor at his house while his wife was out. Taylor later changed his story, saying he had seen Pearl but when she got into trouble after paddling out of reach he, unable to swim, could not rescue the girl.

In court, the police witness read how Taylor, on being charged with the murder, replied, 'I did it because I was frightened of telling her grandmother.' He also spoke of a witness, one yet to come forward, who had seen him and Pearl on the canal and 'may have reported it' but he did not explain further. However, when arrested he produced a penknife and later admitted he had cut the bathing suit but again refused to explain further.

Retiring for just eight minutes the jury returned a verdict of guilty. As the judge donned the requisite black cap he informed Taylor there was but one sentence known to the law. Yet that execution sentence was never carried out. On the last day of 1949 his sentence was commuted to life and Taylor remained behind bars for the rest of his life.

It may seem odd to find a girl of 13 being sent on an errand at 10pm but these were different days and, like the witness Lucy Brent, she was clearly not alone in being abroad at such a time. Just why Taylor's execution was commuted is unclear; some sources state the evidence was largely circumstantial and yet Taylor admitted he had had some involvement. Clearly the victim had met Taylor at least twice before that fateful night, otherwise how could she have known who he was and where he lived when visiting with Betsy Ann?

Reading between the lines, and without any attempt to belittle or detract from the horrendous crime, perhaps the Home Office thought there were other undocumented factors to be taken into consideration.

Conclusion

For more than 200 years the canals have been as much a part of the criminal world as they have of the industrial era and for modern leisure pursuits. For all that time, the dark waters have been a potential dumping ground, particularly during the period before these arteries were reborn as leisure routes.

Even in the twenty-first century, stories continue to surface. At Hartshill, Nuneaton on the Coventry Canal near the Anker Inn, the body of a man was found by a dog walker in the early morning one Easter Monday. Police retrieved the fully clothed body and, following a post mortem, the coroner recorded a verdict of accidental death.

While canals are now kept reasonably free of debris, some smaller items must remain. At around £30 each, the windlass is an expensive lump of metal far too often dropped in the canal. Armed with an underwater metal detector retrieving these could prove quite lucrative, while there must be untold riches in coin hiding in depths. Perhaps even the most valuable of British coins, the one penny coins minted with the head of George V dated 1933 await discovery, its great value down to the assumption that only seven were ever minted.

Surely many thousands of pounds in still-legal tender could also be found. However before handing in your notice we should also bear in mind the significant outlay just to purchase the equipment. Additionally, the many washers and bottle tops which give false signals, will only be discovered after retrieving them from the depths and that is not going to be easy. Furthermore, there will be a fair amount of walking involved.

Some 2,200 miles of canal are found in Britain today. During the heyday of the canal network, millions of tons of cargo was afloat at any one time. The boat would have been of vital importance, often the boatman's home as well as his source of income. Just as a house and car need to be maintained and paid for today, the boat also had to be kept in tip-top condition and, with hidden dangers beneath the surface, repairs were a constant drain on resources.

At the end of the nineteenth century, a boat of oak could be built and fitted out for around £175. While the owner would have part exchanged his previous vessel, that is still a significant outlay and would have been repaid in instalments. Additionally, the vessel had to undergo stringent tests, similar to a modern MOT test on the car, and the vessel would be unlikely to last more than a decade before being replaced.

The boatman leading the horse would have been well aware of the mileage involved in earning a living. While he shared the task, probably with his lady wife steering, he would still have walked many hundreds of miles each year and still have to open and close lock gates, plus help load and unload their boats.

With such pressures, it is hardly surprising to find boatmen were known for heavy drinking, fighting, gambling, and sundry other vices to relieve the strain after work – or sometimes when still working. Under such conditions perhaps even more crime should be expected. Indeed, as this book has shown, there are many crimes yet to be resolved.

We can only guess at how much of the evidence is still to be found at the bottom of the canal. Even more thought-provoking, where will the next piece of vital evidence be dropped and will it be recovered or will the guilty walk free?

Bibliography

British Newspaper Archive
Poulton-Smith, A. (2013) *Paranormal Staffordshire* (Amberley)